AF316694

Poem by Poem, Fable by Fable

Poem by Poem,
Fable by Fable

Discovering My Father and
Learning His Language

Anna Miransky

WIPF & STOCK · Eugene, Oregon

POEM BY POEM, FABLE BY FABLE
Discovering My Father and Learning His Language

Wipf & Stock
An Imprint of Wipf and Stock Publishers
199 W. 8th Ave., Suite 3
Eugene, OR 97401

www.wipfandstock.com

PAPERBACK ISBN: 979-8-3852-1823-3
HARDCOVER ISBN: 979-8-3852-1824-0
EBOOK ISBN: 979-8-3852-1825-7

VERSION NUMBER 06/18/24

Cover image of Yung Vilne logo is owned by the Vilna Gaon Museum of
Jewish History. Used with permission.

To my father, with love and respect for the legacy he left us.
May this book offer a measure of the honor he deserves.

Contents

Bibliography of Peretz Miransky | viii

Biographical Information about Peretz Miransky | ix

Acknowledgments | xi

Introduction | 1

Chapter 1   A Candle for a Penny | 13

Chapter 2   In the Shadow of Yesterday | 34

Chapter 3   Fables | 44

Chapter 4   Creation | 66

Chapter 5   Family | 76

Chapter 6   A Friendship—Chaim Grade | 85

Chapter 7   Within Himself | 92

Chapter 8   Yiddish | 99

Chapter 9   Green Words | 113

Chapter 10   Song of Songs | 124

Afterword | 139

Biographies of Key Figures | 143

Appendix: Poems as Written in Yiddish | 149

Bibliography | 183

Bibliography of Peretz Miransky

- *A likht far a groshn* (A Candle for a Penny), Montreal, 1951
- *Shures shire, lider un mesholim* (Lines of Song; poems and fables), Israel, 1974
- *Tvishn shmeykhl un trer, mesholim* (Between Smile and Tears; fables), Toronto, 1979
- *Nit derzogt, lider* (Incompletely Expressed; poems), Tel Aviv, 1983
- *A zemer fun demer, lider un mesholim* (A Song from the Twilight; poems and fables), Toronto, 1991

Biographical Information about Peretz Miransky

1908   Born in Vilna, Poland, March 24.

1934   Invited to join the Yiddish literary group *Yung-Vilne*.

1939   Leaves Vilna for Vidzy, where he marries and has his first child.

1940   Returns to Vilna with wife and child.

1941   Flees the Nazis.

1941–1944   Survives war in Samarkand, Uzbekistan; meets and marries Lola Bluds.

1944   Returns to Vilna with Lola to search for survivors.

1946   Escapes from Soviet Union and reaches Tempelhof displaced persons camp.

1946   Libi is born in Tempelhof displaced persons camp.

1947   Lives in Paris waiting for immigration papers to Canada.

1948   Sails from Europe to North America. Khane (Anna) is born during the voyage.

1949   Arrives in Montreal.

1951   *A Likht far a groshn* (A Candle for a Penny) is published in Montreal.

1955   Rami is born in Montreal.

1955   Moves to Toronto.

1970   Lola dies, May 25.

1974   *Shures shire* (Lines of Song; poems and fables)
        is published.

1976   Marries Saba Fried.

1979   *Tvishn shmekhl un trer, mesholim* (Between Smile
        and Tears; fables) is published.

1983   *Nit derzogt, lider* (Incompletely Expressed; poems)
        is published.

1988   Receives Itzik Manger Prize for Yiddish poetry.

1991   *A Zemer fun Demer, lider un mesholim* (A Song from the
        Twilight; poems and fables) is published.

1993   Dies in Toronto, July 10.

Acknowledgments

I would like to offer my deep gratitude to three friends for their help in bringing this book to completion:

David Roskies, whose knowledge, commitment and enthusiastic support accompanied me throughout the writing. This book would not have come about without his involvement.

Jared Cappel, whose generously offered editing skills contributed substantially to this book's coherence and vitality.

Jinks Hoffman, whose devotion and effortful engagement pointed me in the right direction.

Introduction

To write about a subject, one should know it well. Yet I did not know my father, the Yiddish poet and fabulist Peretz Miransky, at all well, either as a child or as an adult in the years we had together. A child knows her parents through her encounters with and observations of them. And out of these selected bits of a life—a mosaic of emotionally heightened experiences—she interprets them, creating a picture, which is necessarily incomplete and often distorted by her own needs and grievances.

My most iconic childhood memory with my father is of an event that took place when I was about six years old. Peretz, Papa to his children, asked me if I wanted to learn how to play chess. I nodded eagerly, surprised because he rarely offered me one-on-one attention. We lay on our stomachs on the living room carpet, the chessboard between us. He quickly showed me how each of the pieces moved. He gave me the advantage of the white pieces, and I opened to start the game. It ended in four moves. Papa said proudly, "See how quickly I can checkmate you?" He stood up and walked away.

My father's need to be admired was constant. But there were other sides to him. When I was about ten years old, my mother designated my father to solve the wasp problem in our rented house on Lake Simcoe, a cottage destination an hour's drive from Toronto. I watched as Papa dashed out the front door, pursued by a line of wasps that streamed from a disturbed nest buried in one of the bedroom walls. He scratched his arms, which were covered with red welts, and he laughed, excited about this adventure.

Peretz laughed often. He loved fun, games, and pranks of all kinds, as did everyone else in our family: me; my mother, Lola; my sister, Libi, two years older than me; and my brother, Rami, seven years younger.

By the time I became a psychotherapist, I had developed a rich vocabulary to describe my father. I used adjectives like *needy, boastful, judgmental, self-involved, opinionated,* and *competitive* to describe many of his interactions with me and with others. But I also knew him as fun-loving, energetic, brave, forgiving, and, most importantly, able to acknowledge wrongdoing. I thought that all these adjectives explained him.

I also thought that I had made peace with Peretz. I had, after all, in the months before he died in 1993, sat with him on the sofa in the home he shared with his third wife, Saba, while he read some of his Yiddish poems to me. I penciled English words into the margins of his poetry books, next to the Yiddish words I didn't understand.

At my father's unveiling, I spoke these words, extrapolated and interpreted from a psychological theory[1] I favored at the time: I said that children have two routes by which they can attach to their parents. The first comes from the quality of nurturance, engagement, and care the parents provide, the way the child's needs are seen and responded to. The second comes from who the parent is, whether the child can admire and be guided by the parents' values and the ways these are expressed in the world.

I was saying that although I hadn't been nurtured by or received much attention from my father, I had attached to him by coming to admire him; in particular, the way he had coped with the circumstances of his life as a Holocaust survivor who had lost most of his family and his place in the world. I was saying that I had learned something about spiritual survival from him. I was saying that I had come to peace with him.

---

1. Self Psychology, the first influential psychoanalytic movement recognizing empathy as an essential aspect of human development and growth.

Yet I barely knew the "him" I thought I had made peace with.

All of the adjectives I used to characterize my father described only the waves, not the deep underlying currents. I didn't and couldn't know his depths. When children grow up, they are often able as adults to develop a new and intimate relationship with their parents, coming to a fuller appreciation of who they are as people. But this can be difficult when life is negotiated through two separate languages—English in my case, and Yiddish in my father's. Yiddish was my first language. My parents told me that I spoke it exclusively until I started school at the age of six. I would lose the ability to speak it shortly thereafter.

When I was seven or eight, Papa asked me if I wanted to hear a poem he had just written. I said yes reluctantly. I didn't really know what he expected, but I was the kind of child who couldn't imagine saying no to a parental request. Papa lay on his stomach on his bed, his elbows on the footboard. He read a Yiddish poem to me from a piece of paper in his hand, while I crouched on the floor below, looking up at him. When he finished reading, he asked if I liked the poem. I nodded yes even though I hadn't understood a word.

By the time I was eight, I was answering Papa in English when he spoke to me in Yiddish. This conversational pattern between us would continue for as long as he was alive. My father continued to speak, think, write, and live in Yiddish, while I negotiated life in English.

This could lead to some painful misunderstandings.

Several years after my mother's death from a sudden heart attack in 1970, when I was twenty-one, my father and I had an argument that led to me not seeing or talking to him for some time. After a few anxious and distressing weeks, I called him to apologize. He responded with evident relief and warmth and immediately invited me to dinner with him and his third wife, Saba, whom he married six years after my mother's death. After the meal, he showed me the word *wretch* in a large *Webster's Dictionary* and insisted I had called him that. I explained that this is not a term typically used in modern English-language conversation and not a word I would have used with him or could remember using to describe anyone. To this day, I have no idea what I actually said.

Saba suggested later that evening that the reason Peretz and I argued so often was because we were so alike, a comparison I hotly denied. I refused to acknowledge whatever it was she meant, perhaps a reference to our quick tempers, opiniated natures, or easily injured feelings. And anyway, I insisted, I was more like my mother: both of us musical, emotional, wearing our hearts on our sleeves, and so unlike my father, who showed anger easily, but not vulnerability. I didn't want to be like my father, whom I knew as remote, self-involved, and seemingly uninterested in me.

Despite the misunderstandings, the sound of Yiddish was always in my ears. I overheard my father's conversations in Yiddish, first with my mother, later with Saba, and constantly with friends of the family who came to our home. But I understood these conversations incompletely, and because of that began to tune them out. With the passive Yiddish vocabulary of a young child and my father's broken English, how could we ever have an intimate, meaningful conversation? And so how could I ever really know him?

Compounding the difficulties of understanding one another, a blanket of silence shrouded my childhood home, both about my parents' pre-war lives and about their painful and terrifying experiences and losses during the Holocaust. The stories my parents shared were usually triumphant, involving narrow escapes, lucky breaks, or wily thinking.

My father, for example, told a story about seeking shelter from Nazi bombs in Minsk under an alcove in the street. He gave up his sheltered spot to an elderly woman. A few minutes later, a bomb struck nearby and killed the woman, while my father was spared.

My mother's stories were often given a comic twist. Her tone indicated how we should respond. With exaggerated gestures, laughing, she told of waiting for hours in a ration line in Samarkand to receive a scoop of jam, only to have a street kid swoop in and sweep it from her hand.

There were vast spaces surrounding these anecdotes. Silence about their pasts was a defining characteristic of both my father's and mother's relationship with their children. I knew some basic facts about family members and their fate during the Holocaust, but I knew very little about my family members' pre-war lives.

I picked up information about my parents' pasts by overhearing their conversations with friends or sometimes by interpreting their behavior with me. Around the age of twelve, eavesdropping from my seat on the stairs overlooking our living room, I first learned that my father had a wife and child who perished in the Holocaust.

At around the same age, I learned my mother had a husband before my father when she pointed to a photograph in an album and asked how I would have liked that man, a stranger to me, to be my father. Notwithstanding the inappropriateness of the question and the paralysis it induced, she also failed to tell me the man in the photo had been her first husband, a fact I deduced. I dealt with the question she asked me by adopting my parents' method of silence. Silence about important matters, those that evoked confusion or strong emotion, would become a defining feature of my relationship with them both.

There were still other reasons that I was not particularly close to my father growing up. My mother, Lola, spoke English fluently and was the primary child caretaker. After we moved to Toronto, since my father traveled for work as the subscription manager for a Yiddish newspaper, he was away from home a great deal of the time. Despite these reasons, I interpreted his distance and his lack of engagement in my life as lack of interest and uncaring and didn't push for closeness, taking my own distance from him.

My parents met in Samarkand, where they survived the Holocaust, both having lost their first spouse. My mother's first husband was drafted into the Russian army and was killed on the Leningrad front in 1942 fighting the Nazis. My father's first wife and child were murdered by the Nazis.

My parents came from very different worlds. My father came from Vilna, known as the "Jerusalem of Lithuania" for its rabbinic and Jewish cultural life. Yiddish literature, theatre, and political and educational organizations flourished in Vilna between the two world wars. My mother was from a more assimilated, Russian-speaking family. She had grown up in Riga, went to a German language school, and was proficient in English before she arrived in Canada. Yiddish had not been my mother's native tongue. In fact, she only learned to speak it from my father after they met.

As a teenager, I took my cues about how to view my father from my mother. She and my father seemed to have had a companionable relationship. In their years together, there was little evidence of conflict and he appeared to dote on her.

Yet she could be critical of his table manners, his friends, and his inability to integrate into Canadian culture. When she put on ski pants and a colorful patterned sweater to go to Joso's Café to listen to folk music, it was for an evening out with her closest female friend, not my father. So, the question my mother had asked me about the man in the photo tipped me off to the possibility that my father was lacking in some way. She also didn't seem particularly interested in his Yiddish poetry.

The evidence of my father's preoccupation with poetry was everywhere. Unlike other writers, who reserved a sanctified space or time for writing, every room and piece of furniture contained scraps of paper on which he had written lines of verse in Yiddish. My father wrote constantly, and he wrote when inspiration struck, with whatever material was handy—on the backs of envelopes and flyers and in the margins of newspapers.

I tried to get closer to Peretz in the years after my mother died and he too made an effort, especially after he married Saba. After their marriage, they hosted Friday night family dinners, which included me and my then-partner, Michael; my brother, Rami; his wife, Miriam; and later their two children, Zael and Hayley. I recorded an interview with my father focusing on his wartime experiences during this time.

It was at my request that we sat together on the sofa in his living room in the year before he died to read some of his poetry together. My father chose the poems we read, and in hindsight I would say he chose the easier ones—easier in language, easier in content. But most of his poems and fables remained untranslated and unknown to me, in their closed books lined up on a shelf in my living room. He never asked me if I could or did read them and never suggested that we read them together, although he proudly offered and inscribed a personal message in Yiddish in each newly published book that he gave me.

My father left a legacy of five sizeable books of poetry and fables. Some of these individual poems I heard growing up. He and other Yiddish readers recited these poems at various events: Passover seders, family birthdays, community commemorations, and, later in his life, community celebrations of his literary accomplishments. But even including the poems we read together, I was exposed to only a very small selection of my father's literary output, and I absorbed it without careful attention or complete understanding.

After my father died in 1993, I made attempts to learn Yiddish. I first took a Yiddish course at the University of Toronto in 1997. Then in 1998 I attended a summer Yiddish program in Vilna, his birthplace.

When I returned home, I helped complete a project that my father had begun when he was alive. He had translated some of his poetry into English, from which other writers had crafted English poems. I edited a small volume of these poems and fables, which was published in 2000. I thought that these brief excursions into his poetry helped me know him. What I didn't know about him didn't trouble me very much.

My partner of thirty-five years, Ed Silva, died in 2019, about eight months before the COVID-19 pandemic lockdowns began. I floundered about for a while, grieving, reorganizing, and adjusting to my new single life. During the time I was home alone, like many people, I searched for things to do. I began to study Italian because I was singing in the chorus of an opera company, and I thought that an understanding of Italian would help me learn the opera book I was singing.

Then, from inside, came an essential question: Why was I studying Italian, when I had a language of my own which I knew so incompletely? I looked around for Yiddish courses and decided to start studying Yiddish through the Workers' Circle, a social justice organization that promotes Jewish cultural engagement through Yiddish language learning.

This time, I was studying not solely out of a sense of duty but rather with a commitment that was previously lacking. Shortly after beginning my classes in September 2020, Yiddish words began to spontaneously pop into my head; first isolated words like *bild* (picture) or *groz* (grass), then sentences commenting on what I was doing or feeling, such as *Ikh nem arop di glezer* (I'm taking down the glasses) or *Ikh bin azoy mid* (I'm so tired). I had my first dream in which someone spoke to me in Yiddish, and I responded, *S'iz gut tsu redn a por verter in Yiddish* (It's good to speak a few words in Yiddish).

As I began to think in Yiddish, a forgotten memory came to mind of a game resembling Simon Says that my father played with me when I was a young child. My father would sit opposite me, and I was supposed to lift my hands as he raised his if his question had a yes answer. For example, if he asked, *A meydl vakst?* (Does a little girl grow?), I was supposed to raise my hands. If he asked, *A shteyn vakst?* (Does a stone grow?), I was supposed to sit still. He also asked more creative questions—likely appealing to a poetic mind—which flummoxed me, such as *A shotn vakst?* (Does a shadow grow?).

One day during this first Yiddish course at the Workers' Circle, I received an email from Ida Schiff, a pioneer activist in Yiddish culture and language in Toronto. She asked me to search through my father's books of poetry for a particular poem that Khane Berman, a Yiddish language educator in Toronto, was seeking. I could not find the poem in any of his books. But as I looked through all my father's works, I realized how many of his poems I hadn't read, and I decided on the spot that I would begin a practice. Each day I would sit down and read one poem, until I had read every poem in every book my father had ever published.

I decided to start with his most recently published book, *A Zemer fun demer* (A Song from the Twilight), published in 1991, because this was the book he wrote when my memories of him were most recent. Like most of his books, it includes both poetry and fables, each in its own section. This book begins with poetry. In the very first poem, in a book published two years before his death, I found these closing lines addressing himself, in a poem entitled "*Nekhtn*" (Yesterday):

> Yesterday a dream, a beloved and cherished dream,
> a dream lush and blooming, died.
> So stand upright—like an autumn tree covered with fire
> until the silver winter extinguishes you.

I had no idea to which dying dream this poem referred. Yet the thought of my father dying with an unrealized dream, and the image of him as an autumn tree blazing with color, while accepting his inevitable death, made me weep.

I realized that my father had exposed his soul in his poetry, that this was a way to get to know him, and that it was worth any discomfort I might feel. My father wanted to be understood and I could offer that to him, albeit not in his living presence.

Each day I sat down, usually in the afternoons, with one of his books and my Yiddish-English dictionary. I penciled the English words I did not know into the Yiddish text. It was laborious work; for me, even finding the words in the dictionary was slow and tedious, but I was compelled by what I was reading.

This practice of reading a poem and reflecting on it became a part of my daily life for more than two years. My father—his life, his grief, his losses, his loves, his preoccupations, his pet peeves, his sense of humor—was laid out for me to examine. I began to write down my impressions as they came to me. My understanding deepened as I read and wrote. At times, I had to go back and fill in information I didn't possess when I originally read a poem, but for the most part, I wrote as I discovered.

When it came to organizing this book, I decided on a different structure, grouping my father's writing and my subsequent learning into themes. The first chapter, however, "*A Likht far a groshn*" (A Light for a Penny), is left as I had originally written it, so that the reader might get a sense of my discoveries as I experienced them.

This is a book about the miracle of discovering my father very late in my life, beginning when I was seventy-two. It is also a book about the deep regret that came to accompany my reading and writing. My regret is about what I could not offer my father while he was alive, which I would unreservedly offer him now if only I could—my profound gratitude, deep love, and admiration for the artist he was, for the courage with which he opened and wrote about himself as a Holocaust survivor, for the soul he revealed, and for the artistic and spiritual mission he carried his entire life, which he was unable to see fulfilled. I wasn't aware of this mission—which he defined as the purpose of his life—until I delved into his writing.

My father's books taught me many things: the themes that preoccupied him, the values he held, the ways he thought, the creative and spiritual nature at his core, and his enormous, creative gifts. His writing gave me the opportunity to experience the intimacy I always craved with him. Ultimately, this is a book about how reading my father's poetry and fables changed me and my relationship to him.

Reading my father's poems brought pain, a different kind of pain than the one accompanying me throughout my life. This was not the pain of a lonely child who could not speak to her father and who felt disregarded by and unimportant to him, but rather the pain of a woman who immersed herself in his words and the emotional wounds they revealed and could not console him.

As I read and wrote, I began to find myself in the story. I noticed my own responses, what moved me and what I resonated with. I noticed which themes had the greatest impact on me. I noticed that I was becoming a detective, looking for information about my father's deepest truths, but also about tangible details that were missing in my knowledge of him, particularly details about his life before the war.

Quite early on, I began to mark the poems that made the greatest impact on me, and I knew that some of them would find their way into this book. Through them, I hope to shed some light on an aspect of inner experiences as a child of Holocaust survivors and as a child of immigrants. I hope to show how one can live a whole life incompletely and come to know and embrace one's heritage in the later years of life. I hope to reveal a story of healing, which includes, and has as a requisite condition, a good measure of discomfort and pain.

In Montreal, where we first lived upon arriving in Canada in 1949, I attended the *Folkshule* (the Jewish People's School) in grades 1 and 2, where I acquired my ability to read Yiddish. Toronto had no school teaching Yiddish at the time my family moved here in 1955, except for one my father was suspicious of because in his view its leadership was insufficiently critical of communism. In Toronto, my parents enrolled me in a public school and my Yiddish education ended.

The *Folkshule* in Montreal gave me one other precious gift in addition to the ability to read Yiddish. Dovid Roskies, the distinguished scholar and cultural historian, was my classmate in those grades until my family moved to Toronto. Dovid's mother and my father were both from Vilna. His mother, like my father, revered the richness of Vilna's Yiddish culture, spirituality, and literature.

We rekindled our friendship in 2009, fifty-four years later, when Dovid came to Toronto to speak at the Jewish Book Fair during a tour for his memoir, *Yiddishlands*. Reading it, I felt strongly connected, and we began an email and Skype correspondence. Before I delved directly into my father's work, Dovid was the repository for me of the lost world I was seeking.

When I began to read my father's works seriously, I called on Dovid often for an explanation of a word, custom, or reference I did not understand. From Dovid, I learned where my father's poems and fables fit into the history of Yiddish literature. I learned about his literary forefathers and mentors. I learned why my father was a "modern" Yiddish poet (as will be explained later). I learned to appreciate my father's erudition, vocabulary, and rhythm and rhyme schemes.

Delving into my father's poetry was intensely emotional. But his poems also invited and inspired me to travel, both physically and intellectually—to the YIVO Institute for Jewish Research in New York; to a gravesite in New Jersey; to the work of his literary ancestors; to his friend Chaim Grade's works; and those of the two teachers who most influenced him, Moshe Kulbak and Eliezer Shteynbarg, both of whom are discussed later in this book. In immersing myself in my father's work, I drew closer not only to him, but to the world that inspired him, the world he loved and then lost.

Chapter 1: A Candle for a Penny

My father's first book, *A Likht far a groshn* (A Candle for a Penny), was published in 1950, a year after he and his young family arrived in Montreal, having spent two years in a displaced persons camp in Berlin, where my sister Libi was born, followed by a year in Paris awaiting Canadian immigration documents. My father was forty-two when his book was published. I was one, my sister was three, and my brother Rami was not yet born. A few of these poems were written in Montreal, but mostly this is a collection of poems and fables that were written in Europe, in the pre- and post-war years and during the war itself. He proudly said that he reconstructed them from memory.

Some early poems served as a window into the man he was before the Holocaust obliterated his young life and changed everything. They also added details to his story, which helped me reconstruct his path after escaping from the sphere of Soviet influence. Some of these poems and fables are dated, which allowed me to determine how old he was and what was going on in Vilna and Europe when he wrote them.

A Likht far a groshn (A Candle for a Penny), as a book title, is in itself evocative. It might have been something Peretz heard in the markets of Vilna. It bespeaks something humble but necessary for daily life.

The book opens with an eight-line poem prologue, simply titled *"Mayn lid"* (My Poem), dated Montreal 1950. It translates as follows:

> Although my poem is poor
> like a candle for a penny
> I take pride in its Yiddish language
> and its place on the table.
>
> Not for appearance's sake
> not as a memorial candle
> but right next to a loaf of bread
> and a jug of fresh water.

I found such love poems to Yiddish throughout my father's books. In this one, he expresses how integral Yiddish was to his daily life and spiritual survival.

My first surprise while reading the poetry in this book came from an eight-line poem dated 1933. My father was asked to join *Yung-Vilne* [1] (Young Vilna) in 1934, which was also the year that his first published fables appeared in the *Vilner tog* (Vilna Day, a Yiddish newspaper). I knew that my father's first two published works were fables, I had assumed that fables inaugurated his writing career and corresponded with the year he joined *Yung-Vilne*. But here is a poem written a year earlier, titled *"Dray teg"* (Three Days):

> I have at the bottom of my flooded heart
> three rainbows glowing above threatening clouds.
> As if I were in a wasteland, I track their vestiges
> which lead somewhere, where wonderful is.
>
> And as my life becomes like a ship, in the blue of the sea,
> sailing unanchored from your port
> will I, a pious dervish in my own depths

1. Cammy, "Yung-Vilne."

make a pilgrimage to those days.

Vilna, 1933

The poet at the age of twenty-five has written a love poem to an unknown woman—not to my mother, nor to his first wife, neither of whom he has yet met. I contemplated who she might have been and what about her so entranced my father. Apparently, he was a poet even before he was a fabulist and he reached in his earliest writing for religious imagery to express the holiness and passion of love.

I paid close attention in this first section of poetry, entitled "*Teg*" (Days), to when these poems were written. There is a poem dated 1945, Vilna, entitled "*Es iz mir umetik*" (I Am Uneasy). The war had ended, and my father and mother were in Vilna, now part of the Soviet Union. They traveled to Vilna from Samarkand, where they met and endured the war, to look for surviving family, both having lost their first spouses.

The poem speaks of my father's unrest the moment my mother has departed, even though it has only been a short while. (Presumably, my mother had gone to Riga for a few days to look for surviving relatives.) He wakes up every morning telling himself that she will return the following day. His days, which he likens to tedious guests making an unwelcome visit, mock him for writing such poems to his own wife. But is he to blame, he ponders, that his own heart demands her presence like a hungry child in its cradle? His heart is blind and doesn't see his own greying hair, the hair of a grown man. It knows only its own hunger and unrest.

There has been so much loss that the poet cannot bear this absence, cannot feel ease without the presence of this new love, comfort, and anchor in his life. He likens these dependent feelings to those of a helpless infant seeking its mother's breast.

The next section in the book, also poetry, is entitled "*Milkhome*" (War). These are the poems written during and immediately after the Second World War. Here is my father's wartime history, the information taken directly from an interview I recorded with him in the 1980s.

My father lived with his family in a suburb of Vilna called Shnipeshok between 1924 and 1935. The family had an inn, boarding the horses of surrounding farmers when they came to the Vilna markets twice a week with produce in their wagons. They also earned money from goods, food, and drink they sold to the farmers.

My father's mother, Khane (after whom I was named), died in 1935, and the family business fell apart shortly thereafter, as she had been the mainstay of their enterprise. The Polish government was also taxing Jewish businesses and encouraging the Poles not to frequent them. To make money, my father moved from his parents' house to the center of Vilna and got a job as the manager of a factory producing cigarette papers. This enabled him to send money home to support his family.

My father had become a communist in response to the extreme poverty and difficulties for Jews under Polish authority, believing, as did other Jewish intellectual youth, in the Soviet propaganda about the USSR being a socialist workers' paradise. When the Russians prepared to occupy Vilna in 1939 (under the Molotov–Ribbentrop Pact, partitioning Eastern Europe between the Soviet Union and Nazi Germany), the Polish authorities began to burn their archives. My father and a group of comrades donned red armbands and organized a group that attacked the Polish police and disarmed them.

As a workers' police force, my father and his compatriots welcomed the Soviets when they reached Vilna. But when the Russians transferred Vilna to Lithuania in October 1939, my father was afraid he would be arrested by the Lithuanians for being a communist, and so he left Vilna for a town called Vidzy, 125 kilometers away on the Polish–Russian border.

A merchant there, Lipa Levy, provided financial assistance to people who were arrested for political reasons. My father and two friends, Shmerke Kaczerginski (also a member of *Yung-Vilne*) and Yankel Gotkovitch, were able to shelter with Lipa Levy. My father got a job in Vidzy as a teacher and librarian. He remained in Vidzy for a year, got married there, and had a child.

When Vilna was again under Russian control, my father returned to find work. He got a job as a cultural organizer of unions, then sent for his wife and child to join him.

When the Nazi army approached Vilna in June 1941, my father fled for his life along with many refugees and headed for the Russian border. He knew that as a communist he would be among the first to be executed by the Nazis, but he, like others, including Chaim Grade,[2] did not believe the Nazis would actually kill women and children, and so he sent his wife and child back to her father's home in Vidzy.

At first, he traveled on a horse-drawn wagon, but he gave it to two female friends of his he saw walking on the crowded route toward the border of Russia. He came upon a large vehicle stranded and overheated that needed water. The Russian driver asked him if he knew where to find water. My father brought water from a nearby well, after which the driver offered him a ride.

Once the truck approached the border, it was commandeered by the Russian army and loaded with wounded soldiers. Peretz helped lift the soldiers into the vehicle. He was then told to lie down beside the wounded soldiers and to pretend to be one of them. In this way, he managed to cross the border when so many were stopped and turned back.

My father was headed to Minsk, where his father had relatives. When he got there, he found the city in flames. The highway leading to the next city, Smolensk, some three hundred kilometers away, was crowded with refugees. Russians from Minsk and others fleeing the front were headed there as well, hoping to board a train to take them into the interior. German airplanes were strafing the highway from above and people were struck down as they walked. Seeing this, Peretz abandoned the highway and took side roads, until he reached Smolensk.

As soon as he reached Smolensk, walking on the streets looking for the train station, he was arrested. He was dressed differently from the Russians, wearing a hat and a silk shirt, and according to him, the Russians were on the lookout for spies. He

2. Grade, *My Mother's Sabbath Days*, xi.

was taken to a police station, showed his documents, and was let go. But he kept being arrested and was taken to the same police station eight times.

Finally, the exasperated official ordered a policeman to escort him to the train station and make sure he got on the train. In this way, my father became one of the first refugees to safely reach the interior of the Soviet Union, to Samarkand, Uzbekistan. My father chuckled as he told this part.

A long poem, "*Halbe nakht*" (Midnight), describes a single day there. It is dated 1942, Samarkand, and reads as follows:

> The moon combs a tree on the street corner.
> My cottage is sleeping, like a spot in a frame.
> I wipe the dream from my eyes, pull the day onto my skin
> —a patched shirt—
> and I run to the queue for my bread.

> The night lays ink drops on the silver ground.
> The heavens look down with a thousand eyes.
> I stand in line pressed to a wall,
> a whipped dog
> and my loneliness is mirrored in dark window panes.
> Day breaks, and blues.
> I step closer to the bread with my ration card,
> stretch my hand to the window
> and I don't know if I'm asking or begging ...

> I return with my pound of dark bread.
> Like a wound, the dawn flames red.
> I walk as if drunk, as if lazy.
> And my fingers, like greedy spiders
> tear pieces and put them in my mouth.

> The morning hems white clouds with golden stitches.
> A blond day plays on me and around me.

I carry my tag, a tin number around my neck
to my work group.
I am here with my anguish for twelve hours
stuck to my workbench.
The light from the window is cut into quarters
by the grates that cover them.
The knives gleam like flames
from memorial candles
and human beings sit like destroyed tree trunks
twisted out of their familiar earth.

I sit alone
like a stone
overturned
from the earth
in a dark space.
I am far, I fly far
to my wife and child.
I take apart a chunk of my yesterday
and unravel it.
and my resentment about the world grows
like a poisonous mushroom.

The sun reaches its bloodied head towards the forest.
The distance is on fire.
In the yard, a gang with a crowbar
is wreaking violence
And rejoicing . . .

I drag my cotton life home
to a cottage made of clay.
I come inside my house
say "good morning" to my loneliness,
to the four black walls,

—not my wife
holding my child in her arms.
And I throw my broken head
into my hands, like a brick.
Hope still knocks on my window pane
like a dove with broken wings.
My doubt chases it
like a hawk chases its prey.
My pain screams
like a dark crow
in a destroyed yard . . .

I sit an hour.
I sit two
until sleep, something heavy and solid
rolls me out on the straw mat to rest
and I ask the night, like a naïve child
to at least give me a good dream . . .

How different this poem is from the triumphant tone of the stories my father related about his time in Samarkand, which were full of creative thinking and narrow escapes!

I noticed in this poem, even in the midst of despair, the poet is aware of every flicker of light. I was just beginning to see how my father used light and color in his poems, which hinted to me of a poetic soul moved to reflection by what captured his attention and imagination in the world outside.

As noted in the introduction, I first became aware my father had a wife and child before he married my mother by overhearing a conversation he had with a guest in our Toronto home when I was a child. He told me a detail about his first wife only after my mother died and I started asking more questions, confessing to me that someone told him he was not the father of the child she had given birth to. I don't know why he chose to tell me this piece of information or what to make of it. He may not have known how his wife and child met their fate. He never told me their names. But they, and their place in my father's life, have become more real to me after reading this poem.

Of all the poems I had read to date, this was the most difficult for me to get through, by which I mean it hurt every time I read it. Something in me resonated with the loneliness, which I believe I both "inherited" from my parents and acquired because of their preoccupation with their own inner wounds, leaving them unable to turn their full attention to their children.

I believe inherited loneliness is one of the legacies transferred to children of survivors who are bereft of grandparents, extended family, and an intact and thriving culture. This is by no means intended to compare my experience with my father's; it is merely to acknowledge how wounds get passed from one generation to another, and how trauma appears in the generations after the one who experienced it.

Samarkand, where my father wrote "*Halbe nakht*," was also where my father met my mother. He was by this time a manager of a factory producing shoes for the army. He had been given this position because he found a way of reducing the amount of material needed to make suitcases at a previous factory where he worked. He explained that everyone in Russia in wartime needed to find some way of making extra money, because the money he was given as a worker was eighty rubles a month, enough to buy only a kilo of bread on the black market. Otherwise, workers received a ration of eight hundred grams of bread per day.

My father worked out a scheme for buying leather inserts on the black market. He paid his workers in extra material, thus spurring them to exceed their production quota. His workers used the extra material themselves to make and sell shoes on the black market.

One day he was approached by an acquaintance who told him he knew two young women who had no shoes for the winter. My father brought enough leather for five pairs of shoe soles to a shoemaker who made shoe tops and asked him to make two pairs of shoes in exchange. The shoes were delivered three days later, and my mother and her friend wept with gratitude. In the interview I recorded with my father, he also told me how beautiful she appeared to him.

Including *"Halbe nakht"* (Midnight), the section *"Milkhome"* (War) contains twelve poems, dated Samarkand between 1942 and 1945, Vilna 1945, and Berlin 1946.

"Peretz-lid" (Peretz Poem), dated 1943, is a ballad. It contains several references to I. L. Peretz's work. (A short biographical note about Peretz as well as all other writers mentioned in my father's poetry can be found in the "Biographies of Key Figures" section). *"Peretz-lid"* may have been written after my father heard about the Warsaw Ghetto Uprising in the spring of that year.

In the poem, Peretz, who died in Warsaw, returns to Warsaw to sit *shiva* for his community. He observes the destruction around him and laments to God, saying, "I offered you *dray matones*" (Three Gifts, the title of a martyrological tale of Peretz's). He asks why God has broken *di goldene kayt* (The Golden Chain, the title of Peretz's most famous play). He reminds God that he, Peretz, exalted ordinary Jews and helped them see their spiritual greatness. He asks why God killed those who were full of piety and those who were fighting for justice. He demands retribution and asks who will forge the golden chain when the youngest in the chain were cut down. My father answers Peretz at the end of the poem.

> We will build, we the widely scattered survivors...
> we the students of you, our rabbi,
> will light the torch again, out of the love and truth
> of your golden chain
> of your eternal flame.

My father demonstrates the sophistication of his literary knowledge by including in this ode to Peretz numerous references to his work.

I. L. Peretz, born in 1852, is considered to be one of the three founders of modern Yiddish literature. While exalting Jewish spirituality and piety, he advocated for a shift from religious observance to secular Yiddish culture, to create a strong Jewish national identity apart from religion.

My father, in this poem, states his purpose to continue developing a secular literature in Yiddish, determined that there would be a continuation of people who would understand these literary references and appreciate them. He wishes for there to be a "golden chain" of Yiddish culture and literature that will persist beyond the Holocaust.

I remembered that my father once gave me an English translation of Peretz's short stories from his library. I was in my mid-thirties, preoccupied with my own life, in a new relationship and working a new job. I don't remember being intensely interested in Yiddish at the time. I read one or two stories and then put the book aside.

Now, having read my father's ode to Peretz, I grew curious to read more and looked for the book on my shelf. Opening it, I saw that my father had written an inscription on the fly leaf, which reads: "For Khane, my dear and clever one, the best that I can offer. Peretz' view of *Yiddishkayt*."

I'm not sure which affected me more—the words he used to address me or the words he used to describe what he had given me. "The best that I can offer"! The sentence stunned me. I dissolved into tears when I read these words and his reverence for I. L. Peretz. Still, I realized I had no idea what my father meant by "*Yiddishkayt*." I recognized only that he wanted to share something deep about his connection to his literary roots, and how they still lived inside him. Here was proof, hidden in an inscription in a book I hadn't looked at in forty years.

It was only later, after reading some Peretz, and after conversations with my friend Dovid Roskies (the scholar of Yiddish literature and culture assisting me with this project), that I learned that *Yiddishkayt* is the value system, the ethical core of the Jewish religion, with the ritual aspects considered secondary to living a spiritual life removed. Yiddishists are secular humanists. *Yiddishkayt* combines the ethical essence of the religion with its folk essence, meaning that the principles are derived from the people as well as from the religion.[3]

I also learned that Peretz believed that one must let go of the ritual parts of the Jewish religion that create hatred—for example, the "*Shvoykh khamoshkho*" that is spoken when the door is opened for Elijah, the prophet, during Passover. These words call on God to wreak vengeance on the enemies of the Jewish people. Yiddishists like my father understand that wreaking vengeance is neither humane nor a route to spiritual peace or transcendence.

"*Peretz-lid*" was written during wartime, in 1943. Three of the twelve poems in the "*Milkhome*" section were written after the war had ended, in 1945. Of those, two were written in Vilna itself, then under Soviet occupation, where my father and mother returned to look for surviving family. "*Ikh hob gevolt*" (I Had Wanted) is the first of these and reads as follows:

> I had wanted
> a quiet life, like a rabbi's assistant
> without glory, without wealth.
> Just my days, like peasants with scythes,
> returning from the fields with songs.
> And I would be—your tranquillity
> and you—
> my prayer-book.

> But the flames of sunset
> burnt our home.
> An iron storm
> cut through our young lives,
> and on a tree,
> my yard's chestnut tree,
> my dream was hung
> along with my family.

3. "Yiddishkeit," https://en.wikipedia.org/wiki/Yiddishkeit.

As for me, a speck of dust,
carried by the wind to distant seas,
where shall I go
when distances are blind
and roads have a thousand barriers!

They say the sun has already risen,
that fields are already ripe with new abundance,
that cast iron hail has hailed down.
But through my wandering it has been hard
to encounter my life.
Something in me has split in two
and no metal is enough to solder it together.
My pain trudges in me sharp-cornered
and my rest moans like a wind
torn from chains.

Vilna, 1945

Where could they go? The brutal reality of life in the Soviet Union convinced my father that they had to escape. "Roads have a thousand barriers!" he writes. I knew only that they crossed the border illegally with a guide and that they ended up in the Tempelhof displaced persons camp in Berlin, where my sister, Libi, was born in December 1946.

My mother was pregnant with my sister at the time of the crossing. The poem entitled "*Aliya Bet*" describes the cold dread of this terrible trek. *Aliya Bet* was the term given to the clandestine operation moving Jewish refugees to Palestine when it was under the control of Great Britain. The entire poem is as follows:

A frost, a bony skeleton
embraces the woods with bony fingers;
It is dark, dreadful and still.

Dead waves of barbed wire
form snow-covered hills.
Angry, grey dogs sniff the night, the snow and the wind.

Soldiers stand like a fence
and hold death in their hands . . .
the border between two countries.

Shadows crawl on the snow
a long row, and another row.

Behind them beckons a country road,
a little fire, smoke from the roof,
a bed in a heated house
and they, they crawl slowly ever forward.

They crawl on peeling feet,
with scrapes like cracked nuts,
with blue hands, that bravely write
a fiery document in blood on the snow.

They crawl forward, they crawl, they crawl!
Two borders behind them,
but the road ahead is still long and grey
and the road is covered with snow.

Who are they, where are they crawling to?!

There are no human shoes walking here
not even a wolf passes through here!
Dogs sniff and faithfully follow,
the way a lead bullet follows its aim.
Here, death watches and protects.

Here quiet steps answer
armoured only with belief;
Through seven borders ahead!
Through twenty countries and through cities.
Aliya "Bet"! . . .

1946 Berlin

The phrase *"Aliya 'Bet'"* which closes the poem emphasizes my father's involvement with the group responsible for guiding illegal Jewish refugees out of Eastern Europe to Palestine. I have only this poem to tell me something about this dreadful journey.

The *Mesholim* (Fables) section which closes the book, *"A likht far a groschen,"* takes up about half of the book. There are twenty-six fables in this first book, written in Vilna, Lodz, Paris, and Montreal, the earliest dated Vilna, 1934, and the last Montreal, 1950.

My father, mother, and sister spent a year in Paris in 1947–1948 waiting for the documents that would allow us to come to Canada. My mother was pregnant with me during the Paris spring of 1948. I was born during the Atlantic voyage from Paris to New York in October 1948.

I was eager to read these fables to discover what the poet was thinking when he first began writing in this art form. By now, I understood that my father had been signaling in his writing, both in his technique and in his content, that he stood within a major trend of modern Yiddish literature.

Before Yiddish literature entered modernity, its culture was transmitted orally through songs and performances. In the mid-nineteenth century, modern Yiddish literature traveled in two directions. Some writers embraced modernity wholeheartedly and wrote in all the modalities available in other languages and cultures, such as novels, psychological fiction, expressionist poetry, etc.

The second direction used traditional forms, like songs and fables, but used them to express modern, worldly concerns and ideas. In other words, the early traditional forms were reinvented and used as tools for modern expression. Writers like Itzik Manger,

Sholem Aleichem, and I. B. Singer fall into this category, as does my father.[4] The strengths of these traditional forms are their use of dialogue and performative potential. My father found a natural affinity with the fable form. He chose it, I believe, because it was allegorical and therefore a subversive way of expressing social protest and criticism that would otherwise have been censored. I remember him saying that some of the fables he wrote in Vilna were in fact censored by the Polish authorities.

The fable form also allowed him to express his social observations, judgments, humor, and whimsy. And, as I discovered, he shared a good measure of philosophy and spiritual advice. I believe that my father continued with this form after the Holocaust to maintain his deep connection within the "golden chain" of Yiddish culture. He no longer needed the fable form to express social criticism, but as one of the only fable writers to continue writing in this genre after the Holocaust, he used this form both to express daily and worldly concerns and to honor and continue his deep commitment to maintaining and extending this traditional form of Yiddish literature.

The political satire I found in these fables is veiled. A fable entitled "*Hint*" (Dogs) was placed in *Poyln* (Poland), 1939 rather than Vilna. I assumed this is because it was written in Vidzy. The fable describes how a band of dogs attacks a man out for a peaceful stroll close to a feudal estate. He cries out and is saved by a peasant. With blood running from his wounds, he says that he will denounce and bring an action against the perpetrator. The peasant asks whom he will retaliate against and is told the nobleman from the estate. The peasant tells him that he's obviously not from the area or else he'd understand. The fable ends with this moral:

> And if the nobleman's hounds howl like
> the winds in the fields,
> then perhaps he is no better than
> the dogs.

4. Roskies, "Itzik Manger," 230–65.

The nobleman stands for the authority, most likely the Polish government, that allowed the "dogs" (the vicious local antisemites) to attack the Jews without provocation or compunction.

I became curious about whether there were fables my father had forgotten or had changed from their original versions. So I conducted an internet search to see whether I could locate any of my father's poems and fables that were published in Poland between 1934 and 1939.

I found a total of six fables in this online search, only two of which appear in the writer's first book. These include "*Hint*" (Dogs, discussed above) and "*Di kro un di veverke*" (The Crow and the Squirrel), both of which were published in *Almanakh fun yidishe literatn un zhurnalistn – fareyn in Vilne* (Almanac of the Vilna Association of Yiddish Writers and Journalists).

What struck me was that the two versions of "*Hint*" and "*Di kro un di veverke*" are nearly identical, despite one being written before the war and the other reconstructed after. My father had told me that the poems and fables in this first book were reconstructed from memory, and his memory seems to have served him well.

In "*Hint*" I found minor differences in punctuation and word order from the original to the reconstructed version. A different word for "boss" or "landlord" appears in the original version. Probably most significantly, in the reconstructed version, "nobleman" is modified with *hign,* meaning "local." Perhaps "local" in the original version would have too closely pointed to the neo-fascist Polish authority and led to the fable being censored.

"*Di kro un di veverke*" (The Crow and the Squirrel) also matches closely to the original. It is a very different kind of fable from "*Hint.*" It falls into a category of fables that others have described as "social satire," but which I read as an ongoing discussion about what endeavors or characteristics in a person deserve merit and acknowledgment.

This fable elaborates on that theme by presenting a protagonist, the crow, who criticizes the squirrel for the effort it takes in getting to the kernel of the nut. The crow says derisively that nuts are eaten by rats and mice. The fable ends as fables do, by reiterating the message in the following rhymed couplet:

"It happens when someone wants to
criticize with zeal
they lack the teeth themselves to chew
that kind of meal."

This point about writers' hard work, cultural knowledge, and linguistic sophistication as deserving of acknowledgment and respect are repeated in different ways in many fables. It's probably not a stretch to believe that my father included himself as this kind of writer and wanted the acknowledgment and respect his learning and effort merited.

According to an online annotated blog, "*Di poyk un di fleyt*" (The Flute and the Drum) and "*Di hak un di koyln*" (The Axe and the Coal) were the two fables that introduced Peretz Miransky to the Yiddish-reading public in the Yiddish newspaper *Vilner tog* in 1934. I found "*Di poyk un di fleyt*" in *Literarishe bleter* (Literary Pages), the foremost literary Yiddish journal published in Poland.

In this fable, the flute in an orchestra chides the drum for its incessant noise. The flute says that even the trumpet modulates and mutes its sound to be part of the orchestra. The drum replies:

"It's easy to have a sweet voice when you're
caressed by loving lips and fingers.
But try singing sweetly when someone is
beating your hide!"

This is a theme I encountered again and again, pointing out how differences in circumstances lead to differences in behavior. It expresses the universal sense of outrage felt when one's life is full of abuse and injustice.

In *Literarishe bleter*, I also found a fable, entitled "*Der shaytl holtz un der toperiske*" (The Piece of Wood and the Axe Handle). This one, like "*Di hak un di koyln*" (The Axe and the Coal), does not appear in any of my father's books. I read it with great curiosity.

The axe handle finds itself in the proximity of a piece of wood in a rich man's home. It recognizes that they are both from the bark of the same maple tree, brothers, garbed in the same shirt, descendants from the same mother and father. It asks the piece of wood why it is so unfriendly. The piece of wood answers in a straightforward manner: "Do you know why you are so repugnant to me? It's because when you're given a hat of steel, you follow the hands that send you to murder your brothers!"

This fable along with one entitled "*Left-gopl*" (Spoon-Fork) were published in *Literarishe bleter*. "*Der shaytl holtz un der tope-riske*" (The Piece of Wood and the Axe Handle) was published in February 1937, managing to get past the Polish censors. It seems directly aimed at collaborators with murderous regimes. It led me to speculate about whom my father might be referring to when writing about a tool becoming emboldened to do murder at the hands of another. Hitler and Mussolini were both in power at this time. Germany signed a ten-year non-aggression pact with Poland in 1934. And throughout history, there have been individual informers and collaborators betraying others for their personal gain. As someone who shared my father's political sensibilities, I wish he were here so that I could ask him to whom this fable referred.

It's possible that the writer didn't remember the three omitted fables at the time he was constructing his books, although in the case of the two published in *Literarish bleter* that seems unlikely. Again, I can only speculate on why they were not included.

The fable "*A likhtl*" (A Candle) closes the fable section and ends the book. In reviewing this fable, what is most striking to me is the writer's respect for and deep understanding of Jewish religious practices. My father received a traditional religious education. Until the age of twelve, he attended *heder* (religious elementary school). He studied under the Vilna Rabbi Abe Kesl, after which he completed *Herzliya* High School, a secular school that allowed him access to the *Strashun* library.[5] He grew up in a religious home with a very devout father. Around the holiday table with family and friends, my father was always the one

5. Zalkin, "Strashun, Shemu'el and Matityahu"

nominated to lead the service. His knowledge and confidence in doing so were apparent.

His communist ideals, *Yidishkayt*, and the Holocaust may all have had their parts in causing my father to turn away from his religious upbringing. His children had virtually no religious education or exposure. My parents did not maintain a kosher home. We didn't celebrate Shabbat or practice the ritual aspects of any of the religious holidays. In addition to the traditional bottles of borsht and *shchav* on the refrigerator shelves, my father also brought home butcher paper parcels of wrapped *shinke* (ham). He and Saba both had strong judgments about religious Jews who put on a show of piety but behaved immorally.

In "*A likhtl*" (A Candle), a rabbi awakes at midnight, performs ritual handwashing, lights a small candle, and sits down to prepare for the practice of *khtsos*. (*Khtsos* is the pious, mystical, Kabbalistic practice of arising at midnight for study and prayer in memory of the destruction of Jerusalem. Performing this practice is a sign of exceptional piety). The fable continues:

The wind begins to blow and the candle begins
to cry with tallow tears.
She is punished with this fate.
She had dreamed and hoped to be a Sabbath candle.
If she were a Sabbath candle, a mother with two transparent hands
would cover her face and whisper a prayer over her.
A father just come in from synagogue
would say the blessing over wine next to
her glowing light
over two loaves of Challah.
And at her feet on a chair,
a child, full of amazement would chatter.
She could calmly live out her life, layer after layer
and would flicker as is a candle's destiny.
On a tablecloth, in a candlestick . . .

But here, in the middle of the night, in the damp
next to a weeping Book of Lamentations
where a rascal, a breeze, comes to make her flame flicker
and in its whirl, bend her body—
That's too much!

Let a storm descend on all the houses
and hurl this crooked table,
the country of her sick life.
She would throw herself on the holy book, on the floor and walls
and burn up everything in a huge, red conflagration
until the whole shtetl is burned to ashes! . . .

SSSSSSSHHHHHT!
The holy book turns its page
like an unfettered tongue;
"Don't ask for a storm, sister!"
The truth
If you burn everything down,
it will extinguish all the light . . .

The candle, bemoaning her fate, has most of the lines in this fable. The message seems to suggest "be careful what you ask for." The poet explains that revolution exacts a terrible price. My father had become a communist as a protest against and as means to eradicate the poverty and the injustice he and his community lived with. As an idealistic young man, he believed in the dream of equality and justice for all. He saw the broken dream up close in his years in Samarkand. He pays his deep respect to the religious traditions and practices that were prohibited and destroyed in the Bolshevik revolutions. That he closed his first book with this fable is a powerful statement of unbelief and belief.

Chapter 2: In the Shadow of Yesterday

Each of my father's poetry books has a section devoted specifically to the losses of the past. Except for the first, called *Milkhome* (War), written during and immediately after the war, these book sections reveal the impact of the Holocaust on my father's later life. They are labeled consecutively "*Lider fun shotn*" (Poems from the Shadow), "*Shotns fun nekhten*" (Shadows from Yesterday), and "*In shotn fun nekhtn*" (In the Shadow of Yesterday).

My father never escaped the "shadows of yesterday." Although many writers focus on the past, these shadow poems were a direct attempt to remember, grieve, memorialize, and grapple with catastrophic loss.

Reading all these poems together was a revelation, a study in loss. My father wrote about his personal losses, including his sisters and brother who perished. He wrote about the loss of his home, his street, and his community. He described the water carriers, the woodcutters, and the sights and sounds of the markets. He wrote about those who perished in the ghettos and camps and the absence of gravestones where family members could go to grieve their loss. He wrote about losing poet and writer friends who were killed in the Soviet Union. He lamented the loss of the place that poets once held in his culture and the end of the literary group *Yung-Vilne* to which he had belonged. He mourned the Yiddish writers who died in his after-war lifetime. He grieved the loss of the person he had been.

The shadows of these chapter titles are not only the shadows of death and destruction. They are also the shadows of guilt and self-recrimination. My father wrote about the mistakes of his youth and how he had hurt his parents. He described his guilt at surviving when so many others perished. He wrote about shadows being all that remained inside him from a once-vibrant life.

I came upon the first shadow poems early in my reading, fearfully, because I knew they would penetrate me and leave me feeling shaken. Poems written almost fifty years after the Holocaust revealed the still-aching wounds of the irretrievable loss of home.

Sometimes after reading one of these poems, I needed to walk for hours to regain my equilibrium. My feelings were complicated. I felt grief for what my parents were robbed of and what I was robbed of in turn. I felt compassion for my father's pain and regret for what I hadn't seen when he was still with me.

Unlike my mother, who suffered obvious periods of depression throughout her life, my father usually appeared full of energy, vigorous and alive. I misunderstood the depths of his ongoing grief. I remembered my surprise one time when my mother queried him about why he continued to visit a particular family that she found uninteresting. He answered that he liked to visit them because they also came from Vilna, simply to be with others who shared his memories. These were *poshete mentshn* (simple unassuming people), a phrase my father used to describe people who were unsophisticated and didn't put on airs, but able to give my father a great deal because of their common origins and shared memories.

Despite both of my parents' efforts to shield their children from their pain, the darkness inside them penetrated me. I have been drawn to darkness my entire life. Darkness is home, familiar. I've always been acutely aware of suffering despite not fully knowing the context. I became a psychotherapist, in part, I believe, to fulfill my need for emotional intimacy, to give to others what I needed the most: connection, emotional understanding, and companionship in the places that are deeply painful. I worked for many years with survivors of childhood abuse, with some people tortured to such an extreme that they had to dissociate to escape reality.

I've learned from grappling with my own inner darkness that the vast emptiness of loss and disconnection can be partially filled with feelings. It is not a substitute for a home, a country, a culture, a community, or a language, but our feelings felt can keep us spiritually and emotionally alive.

While I always longed to express my feelings to others in intimate personal encounters, my father did it his way. He was a poet, and so his writing was the vehicle in which he expressed his deepest truths and feelings.

Like so many other Yiddish writers, my father, who had his own version of spirituality, addresses God in his poetry, as if he is interrogating the source of the persecutions that have befallen the Jewish people throughout history. His poems contain references to destruction perpetrated from ancient times by people such as the Philistines and Amalekites to the horrors perpetrated by Nazi Germany and the Soviet Union. When he addresses God, it is to vent his rage at injustice, at the slaughter of innocents, at the destruction of a people and culture, at the way the world is.

A long poem in the section *"Shotns fun nekhtn"* (Shadows from Yesterday) is entitled *"A kiddush"* (A Blessing over Wine). It takes place during Passover. My father opens the poem by asking God to forgive him for speaking to him in Yiddish rather than from the Haggadah (the text recited at the Seder on the first two nights of Passover, which includes a narrative of the exodus). He says God deserves praise for freeing his people from Egypt, but then speaks his grievances against God for having allowed the endless persecutions that followed through the ages. He asks if it always has to be this way, if we have to praise God wherever God is despite these terrible tragedies God has permitted.

He argues that when God has inscribed a beautiful and just world, in which all people "brown, yellow, white and black" are brothers, then our prayers will come not from the prayer book but willingly from a gladdened heart. He goes on to describe himself as a man from an abandoned generation who day and night is not free of yesterday's nightmares. His generation shines "like dead stars." He adds, "with all the pain we carry, it's a wonder we are not insane."

Although as a young man my father abandoned traditional religious life and as a poet he raged against God, his poems showed me that he loved and respected the pious morality of his parents, the spiritual generosity of his mother and grandfather, and the ancient religious practices and traditions of Judaism.

An ongoing shadow, or source of grief, in his writing is his relationship with his devout father. In "*Tate mayner*" (My Father), he speaks directly to his dead father:

> My dead unforgotten father,
> resting far away in Vilna all alone
> like a red burning tree, in autumn,
> you burn anew in my flesh and bones.
>
> There wasn't peace between us,
> we were both stubborn;
> and the stubbornness divided and parted us,
> but now father, I wear your face.
>
> All the words you preached to me
> in the old, distant simple days
> return to me now, inherited,
> greening in the plot of my mind.
>
> Now father, I think your thoughts
> when I hear my children speaking,
> when I see them taking earthly paths,
> seeking the earthly Garden of Eden.
>
> I too rebelled in my youth
> against God, against the life you led.

I dreamed that my gaudy banner would wave
over the entire world.

But my cherished beliefs
died with the new moon,
and a gleaming knife of steel
slaughtered my dream on the white snow.

My father, I am still investigating and examining
the errors of my younger life.
I argue exactly as you did once with
the younger generation,
the stubborn, long-haired ones.

Now I hear your long-ago complaints
planted and sprouting in my thoughts,
illuminated like cloudlets
in my yellow autumn evenings.

My dead father, dying too early
lying far away in Vilna all alone,
like a red burning tree in autumn
you burn anew in my flesh and bones.

The repetition of the first and last lines, the use of the Yiddish word *vider* ("again" or "anew," as I have chosen to translate it), and the metaphor of the red burning tree tell me of the heat and turmoil in the struggle between my father and my pious grandfather, alive again in his thoughts in his last years of life. The poem is not dated but appears in my father's final book, *A zemer fun demer* (A Song from the Twilight), published in 1991, two years before his death.

There is much to digest in this poem, including my father's guilt for taking up the communist banner and his profound disillusionment in what ensued. It is one thing to struggle and part ways with the previous generation but quite another to destroy a cherished relationship for an ideal that proved so false and destructive.

My father wrote about the inner need to remember and convey his losses to the Jewish community when it no longer wanted to hear about them. He complained about people who believed that a yearly memorial was an adequate response to the catastrophe.

He contrasted his own losses with the community's response to the Holocaust in his emblematic poem "*Vayse toybn*" (White Doves), dated March 1977.

In it, the poet uses colors—the growth of green and the purity of white snow—to describe his thirty-four years of life in Vilna before the war. He also uses the color white to describe his sisters' purity and beauty as "white doves" murdered, as well as to describe the indifferent response of the universe, as "cold white stars" shining above their burnt nests.

In bitter outrage, he curses the slaughter of his sisters and the fact that the world is forgetful of the pain of the survivors. When he closes his eyes at night, he sees images of neighbors laughing, mocking the destruction of his home and the murder of his brother. He writes that his heart is now as empty as a broken-down house. All that remains in it is an image of his mother, dressed in black, who wanders in the abandoned house as if compelled to be there.

He wonders who he should tell all this to when the world has already forgotten the catastrophe that left him alive. He is ashamed that he has already forgotten some of the names of the dead. He feels guilty that he has survived and is not lying alongside the scattered bones of the dead. He, however, has no choice. Someone has planted within him the "last scream" of the victims lest he forget their pain, so that he will say Kaddish in Yiddish and "in *Kanadish*" (Canadian) until his last breath.

A scene reiterated many times in my father's poetry is the ruined site of his former home, to which he returned after the war—his modest, beloved, and memorialized home. I learned from his poetry that it was a small wooden cottage near a tollgate in the countryside, with two birch trees in the front yard. When I travelled to Vilna in 1998, I tried to find my father's street, but like most signs of Jewish life in Vilna, it had been obliterated during the fifty years of Soviet occupation. A plaza and four-lane road had been built through the area where my father's cottage once stood.

My father's despair about the continuity of his literary inheritance is laid out in a poem on the fiftieth anniversary of the foundation of *Yung-Vilne*. As he often did in memorial poems, in "*Fuftsik yor yung-vilne*" (Fifty Years, Young Vilna), he first paid tribute to what had been. I had learned much more by now about my father's literary group *Yung-Vilne* and the creative, collaborative, idealistic atmosphere that nurtured it. In this memorial poem, he writes that a young generation sprang up from poverty, but imbued with inspiration, they created their own music. The city shimmered in light then and summer days rushed by. When *Yung-Vilne* put out its inaugural issue of poems, the sound was like a flag fluttering, dispersing its music and inspiring others.

Then, as in many of my father's poems, comes a shift in direction. What was is no longer. He describes a brown snake from the west winding itself around half a world. "It scorched the fields with poison and set fire to Jewish towns like haystacks." Half of the members of *Yung-Vilne* were killed and the remainder "flew like birds to other lands." And even in flight, in the "dense forests of Lithuania" and in the "red land which they were faithful to," they were slaughtered.

He writes that only three from *Yung-Vilne* remained alive, to sing their unfinished songs, to pen their unfinished writings. "We are reciters of Kaddish now," he writes, "old men, grey and tired, yet we still bear this testament to the world." He ends the poem with a question: "Who will inherit from us three, we who have lost all our goods in a conflagration?"

Yung-Vilne was officially established on October 11, 1929, so this poem must have been written in 1979, when the three remaining members of *Yung-Vilne*—my father, Avrom Sutzkever, and Chaim Grade—were still alive. Grade died in 1982, my father in 1993, and Sutzkever, the longest-surviving member of *Yung-Vilne*, in 2010.

Because my father's mourning was concealed from me, hidden behind a façade of normalcy, I misunderstood the extent of his pain my entire life. But in his poetry, his heart is a broken house and his body is a broken bottle filled with ash, a tombstone and a coffin. When night approached and his defenses were down, the scenes of the greatest trauma burned into my father's brain came back to haunt him.

I read "*Ikh bin geven*" (I Was) as another kind of mourning poem, this one for the person he had been and could never be again. It reads:

> I was a cedar tree in a forest of green singers,
> a sap-filled cedar, from a bright past.
> I used to stretch out my needle-fingers to the skies
> and light them up in the dawn of every morning.
>
> I stretched to my fullest height, to the stature
> of my grandfathers,
> the elders with their sunny heads and shadowy beards;
> I rocked my crown with theirs on sky swings
> and tied my feet to the simpleness of earth.
>
> Around me stood a forest that whispered and
> spoke my language
> and its floor greened with saplings and with sorrel.
> At night a shower of stars extinguished themselves
> on my shock of hair
> and left lines of mysterious writing on my head.
>
> The moon covered me in silver like a lyre while I rested
> and tuned the strings, my branches, my green branches.

Like birds, words would nest on me,
and my youth swayed in the flutter of my language
set to music.

But an axe, a murderer's axe cut me from my trunk
and skinned the bark from my pale body,
and left me naked in the middle of a foreign world
tied to a wire net, standing on the outskirts of life.

Now I am a telephone pole on sunset steppes.
I stand beside where life is, without my branches,
a cripple.
The hacked off branches sway in my yesterdays
and cry out of me to the serene world.

The transformation from his beginnings as a cedar tree in a forest of young singers to his present life, as a telephone pole, cut down by a murderer's axe, naked and alone in a foreign world, is a bleak and painful one. He says he used to be joyfully growing and flourishing, connected to his ancestors and community. Now he feels like a dead piece of wood, taken from his surroundings, deposited in a foreign world, an onlooker rather than a participant in life.

The theme is a kind of loss that should have its own vocabulary. It is a loss of personal destiny, of the person he remembered himself to be, torn from the surroundings in which his destiny was to be lived out, the place in which he and his gift were nurtured and flourished and meant to grow.

As always, my father's despair about his losses, including the person he was and the continuity of his literary inheritance, refused to be his last or only word on the subject. He closes a section entitled "*Vertershaf*" (Word Creation) with a poem called "*Lekhayim*" (To Life). In this poem, my father begins by grieving his former capacity to fly without wings. He writes that he has even heard a young rainbow sing and yet all these glories bequeathed to him are tinged with woe. Pain accompanies every one of his Yiddish hymns. His words bloom like red poppies but he has no one to gift his treasures to. He has spent a lifetime polishing and purifying his language. Yiddish is his beauty and his adornment and is still the light in his being.

He asks himself, with tears, for whom he so polishes and extolls the language, and to whom he can leave this inheritance. He hurries because he knows that winter will come soon, and the waves that move within him will become frozen.

My father had once lived with a sense of purpose, shoulder to shoulder with other young writers, developing new forms of writing, breaking the traditions of their parents, seeking to create a new world, writing the hymns that would inspire their people to see beauty within and without and to fight for justice.

But for whom is he writing after experiencing such losses? He asks himself this question often. He answers—finding his wisdom as he so often did—in nature:

It is for the lilac that sleeps in the winter when
the earth is frozen
and wakes up in the spring to the great reckoning.
One can already see the wisps of grass in
the garden beds,
the heirs of faded songs.
So what if I am already old and it is already late,
and the noisy street does not hear me?
In the spring a fresh poet will sprout from my old songs.
Then my name will be young again and will be renewed
in the other's poems.
And like old wine, a good drink, my poems will be
toasted with *Lekhayim.*

Chapter 3: Fables

My father is known in the Yiddish literary world as a writer of fables, the artistic form in which he made his debut as a writer on February 2, 1934, first in the Yiddish newspaper the *Vilner tog* (Vilna Day) and later in the literary journals and newspapers in the surrounding cities and towns of Poland.

Until the beginning of Word War II, he was published in the Warsaw-based *Literarishe bleter* (Literary Pages) and *Almanakh* (Almanac) of the Vilna Jewish Literary Association, as well as Kovno's *Naye bleter* (New Pages) and *Emes* (Truth). His fables were reprinted in newspapers in Bialystok, Grodno, and beyond.

The fable typically has two protagonists from the natural world, often animals. These protagonists, more often than not antagonists, are vehicles for expressing the writer's moral stance. Rich is pitted against poor, a wise creature versus a fool, a crafty person versus a naïve one. They are all animated, with voices and opinions, and used to contrast two divergent points of view. Sometimes the narrator or a third character comments on or resolves the argument. The fable typically ends with a pithy moral, to make sure the point is driven home.

My father often said that one of his two major influences and teachers was Eliezer Shteynbarg. Shteynbarg (1880–1932), born twenty-eight years before my father, was the first in the Yiddish literary world to take the ancient fable form and legitimize it as a tool of modernist Yiddish writing, bringing a critical and original perspective to modern issues.[1] And as my father discovered for himself, the fable was a flexible form that could subtly and subversively express some of the political themes that would otherwise be censored.

As the story goes, my father once heard the actor Hertz Grosbard, in one of his famous "word concerts," reading Shteynbarg's fables and was so taken by them that, upon coming home, he wrote his first two fables. My father often told the story of how his friend the poet Shimshon Kahan, the assistant editor of *Vilner tog*, once noticed a notebook sticking out of his shirt pocket. He grabbed it and ran. The next day, my father was astonished to see two of his fables published in this newspaper.

I remember my father saying that he was the only writer of Yiddish fables to survive the Holocaust. Apparently, this is not true. I was able to find two others. Leyb Olitski, a prolific writer of poetry, fables, and short stories, acclaimed for a book of fables called *Mesholin far kinder un groyse* (Fables for Youngsters and Adults), published in 1929, also survived the Holocaust and also wrote fables after the war. But inevitably, given that he was living post-war in the Soviet Union, Olitski turned away from the natural world and wrote fables in an urban setting to highlight themes of inequality and social injustice. Although my father lived in an urban setting for more than half of his life, the great majority of his settings remained in the natural world in which he was born and developed as a young man.

The other fable writer who survived the Holocaust, Yitskhok Goldkorn, was mentioned in one of Chaim Grade's letters to my father. In that letter, Grade explained that the *Forverts* (The Jewish Daily Forward) newspaper was unwilling to publish my father's fables until Goldkorn (who was at the time very ill) had passed away. There was no other explanation given. As his biographical note indicates, Yitshok Goldkorn had been a staff writer at the *Forverts*.

It was not in fact until 1988, when Goldkorn died, that my father became the only Holocaust survivor still writing fables. He

1. Niborski, "Shteynbarg, Eliezer"

continued writing them up until and including in his last book, published in 1991. Every one of his five published books except one, *Nit derzogt* (Lines of Song), which was devoted entirely to poetry, has a section of fables in it.

As was already noted in chapter 1, my father, living in Vilna, then part of Poland between the two world wars, used the fable as a vehicle to protest social injustice and comment on the human cost of inequality and injustice. My father's fables were described by critics as "social satire." But even in his earliest fables, as in "*Di kro un di veverke*" (The Crow and the Squirrel), written in Vilna in the 1930s, my father was already using the fable form to express a theme on which he elaborated throughout his life: what is worthy of merit in a person and in art?

One of my first realizations, reading my father's fables, was how so many of the settings of his fables were from the country-side surrounding Vilna, rather than from the natural world that surrounded him here in Canada. It was not surprising to me that so many of the fables in his first book, *A likht far a groshn*, which was published in Montreal in 1951, were set in the natural world surrounding Vilna, as most of those fables were reproduced from memory and originally written while in Vilna. But it did surprise me to find the world of Vilna and its surroundings still so strongly represented twenty-five years later in his second book, *Shures shire* (Lines of Song), published in 1974, and in his later books as well.

Like Shteynbarg, my father adapted the fable form to address modern-day concerns. But I came to believe that his continuing to write in this form, not only advanced his goal of perpetuating this form and retaining a link in the golden chain of Yiddish literature, but also kept him connected to what he so loved and missed—Vilna—his daily life there and the countryside outside his window. He could imaginatively revisit Vilna in this form—in its terrain, wildlife, characters, everyday tools and implements—and he could reconnect with the landscape that was so familiar and beloved.

In my father's fables, it seems that his two protagonists could be anything at all besides animals: plants, sacks of grain, buckets, candles, salad bowls or clouds, to name some. Some characters that appear in his fables written in Canada—like bellows and coals, wells and water carriers—existed only in his life there, in his native suburb of Vilna, Shnipeshok.

Raised in an urban environment myself, I was particularly struck by how much of the animal and natural world was familiar to my father. There is an abundance of trees, flowers, vegetables, and herbs named and elaborated upon in his fables. He describes what they looked like, where they grew, and how they developed. Some of the trees, like birch, pine, fir, and chestnut, are familiar to me, although I'm sure I wouldn't be able to tell the difference between pine and fir, for example, or recognize a chestnut tree without its pods. Other trees, like linden and alder; flowers like asters and catkins; and herbs like wormwood, myrtle and spikenard; stymied me completely.

Aside from the squirrels, moths, butterflies, bees, worms, ants, mice, dogs, tomcats, sparrows, ravens, crows, swallows, rabbits, horses, turkeys, ducks, roosters, and hens seen by my father both in Canada and in Lithuania are the pigs, billy-goats, donkeys, oxen, storks, eagles, peacocks, and nightingales from his memories of Vilna. These creatures serve in my father's fables as actors, victims, and commentators. They are described with the detail that is only possible with direct observation.

In addition to retaining some of the protagonists and surroundings of Vilna, even after he had been in Canada for twenty-five years and more, my father continued to use fables to reflect on and reveal his moral concerns and values and answer the question of what deserves merit and acknowledgment, in one's character and in art.

According to the fabulist, what is not worthy are unscrupulous rich people and those who revere them despite their crimes. He criticizes greedy people who would steal the sun if they could, outward shows of piety that could hide sins, and talking a good game while being stingy. Clearly, wealth and insincere displays are not the measure of worth, according to my father.

What then is deemed worthy according to these fables? A good heart, humility, quiet generosity, not putting on airs. What is worthy of respect and admiration in art? The willingness to persevere despite frustration and hardship, the hard work necessary to achieve perfection in a creative task, the depth of knowledge that one brings to the creative process, the fruits of hard labor.

A theme that appears repeatedly is the contrast between what one presents to the outside world as compared to one's inner spiritual core. Colorful butterflies who flit from blossom to blossom and flirt with all flowers are essentially "worms with painted wings." One can be talkative, like the tongue, even aggressively opiniated, and not be "wrong," while the teeth, who are silent and don't say anything offensive, can hide rot underneath their gold fillings.

As a writer and a human being, having "deep roots" was a requirement for my father. Two very different fables elaborate on this theme. One is "*An antene*" (An Antenna), which is clearly set in contemporary times, here, in Canada. An antenna is haughty and thinks it is incomparable because of its height and its shininess. From its position, rooted in an attic, at the corner of a roof, it mocks a nearby cherry tree, which provokes the antenna's ire because of its beauty. The antenna mocks the tree because it stands in the mud and its feet are in the ground, among the worms, yet it stretches its arms to God. The antenna adds that achievement requires intelligence and if one has it, one attains the heights. Possessed of intelligence, one isn't stuck in the earth like the cherry tree, where the wind rocks its lame branches and they merely obey. The cherry tree answers, addressing the antenna as "Mister Preacher!" The poet continues:

What is haughtiness?
Just a whitecap on a wave over an abyss.
You are held in a harness, inert on a crooked roof,
without a stem, without a core, without a root.
What worth does height have when you don't
bring forth fruit?
What worth does your polish have, if you praise
only yourself?
Those who cannot descend to the depths
cannot elevate themselves.

"Deep roots" refers to authentic, earned knowledge gained from in-depth study, as compared to shallow, superficial showing off. This theme resurfaces in a lighter way in "*A Moshl mit an akhbroshl*" (A Fable About a House Mouse), translated by Hindy Nosek-Ableson below:

At the home of Chaim Ora
a pious scholar steeped in Torah,
a little mouse snuck in and crawled
into a cranny in his wall.

It nibbled on some ancient pages,
filled with wisdom of the ages,
tender morsels of *Gemorah*
mixed with *Khumash! Keyn eyn hore!*

Craving something else to eat,
he went to live across the street,
where he satisfied his hunger
at the shop of grocer Unger.

There he found so many treats,
wheat and sugar, cheese to eat,
barrels full of grain and rice
and a charming group of mice.

Stomach full and back to healthy,
feeling satisfied and wealthy,
he began to quote out loud
in a voice assured and proud.

From the hole came words so wise,
they lit up all the mice's eyes.
Parables and laws from Torah,
quotes from *Khumash* and *Gemorah*.

Complete chapters, edicts, laws.
Applause! Applause! They licked their paws
and wagged astonished little tongues.
"A miracle—from one so young!"

What a rodent, what a sage!
After nibbling one small page
of *Khumash* and a smidge *Gemorah*
He is teaching "*Sitre Torah*."

The expression *keyn eyn hore* (literally, no evil eye) is meant to neutralize evil spirits or bad luck, usually when something positive is said. It is the Yiddish equivalent of "knock on wood."

Khumash refers to any one of the five books of the Torah, the five books of Moses. The *Gemorah*, collected in sixty-three volumes, is one of two essential components of the Talmud (Mishnah and Gemorah) and is the compilation of rabbinical commentaries comprising Jewish religious law. *Sitre Torah* translates as "secrets of the Torah" and refers to the esoteric, mystical teachings in the Torah. In traditional Jewish study, immersion in these teachings would be undertaken only by mature and serious students with a solid foundation in both the Torah and rabbinical commentaries.

Given these necessary annotations, a few words about translation from Yiddish to English might be useful here. In general, fables are easier to translate from Yiddish to English than poetry is. The fable describes an interaction, rather than trying to illuminate an experience. In so doing, it uses more everyday, conversational language. It is therefore easier to preserve the rhythm and rhyme of the original Yiddish in the English translation.

"*A moshl mit an akhbroshl*" (A Fable about a House Mouse) does a good job of capturing in English the playfulness and humor found in the original Yiddish. Nevertheless, in order for the translation to preserve the meaning and the rhyme, the names of the Hebrew/Yiddish texts, likely unfamiliar to anyone without a traditional Jewish religious education, must also be preserved.

Yiddish, like Russian, has a strong tradition of rhyme in poetry. My father's Yiddish poetry and fables rhyme without exception. He rhymes words from Yiddish both with other Yiddish words but also with words derived from Hebrew and from the Slavic languages. When these rhyming pairs were chosen, they were meant either to emphasize the holiness of an idea, provide an ironic commentary or comic effect, or root the experience in a particular place.

When translating his poetry, I chose to sacrifice the rhyme to preserve the essence of the poem as best I could; in other words, to preserve the poetry of the poem. What is lost in the English translations are the rhythm and rhyme of the poem as well as the layers of meaning provided by a well-chosen rhyme in Yiddish. In some of these Yiddish poems, those additional meanings are available only to readers of Yiddish who are familiar with Jewish religion and history as well as with Yiddish literature. Those additional meanings disappear in English translation. Those poems and fables must be annotated. Although annotation provides information, it can never replace the magic of a well-chosen rhyme. For comparison purposes, the original poems in Yiddish that were translated into English for this book are provided in an appendix at the end of this book.

As I read my father's Yiddish poetry, when looking up words and learning how to translate them, I discovered terms describing rituals and practices that I was completely unfamiliar with. Yiddish is very rich in words from *loshn-koydesh* (the holy language, Hebrew). Although my father abandoned traditional religious practice, those words remained available to him, as part of his Yiddish vocabulary. His familiarity with these words and terms allowed him to use them flexibly and playfully. He brought this rich spiritual vocabulary to life by using it in a secular context, which he did extensively in his fables.

Lacking a traditional Jewish education, I was unfamiliar with many of those words before starting this process. Had I retained and developed my first language, Yiddish, these words and practices would have been part of my vocabulary.

In order to fully understand my father's poetry, it was necessary to understand his Yiddish vocabulary, an endeavor that was far more onerous than simply learning words. Accessing the poet's vocabulary through discussion and study provided me with another way of accessing the world that was lost. In other words, through discovering my father's poetry and fables, I discovered more of his world, simply by becoming more familiar with his vocabulary.

My father's earliest themes remained lifelong concerns and were explored from different perspectives, in different scenarios, with different characters, and in different moods. He frequently explored the theme of pretension through snobbish characters exhibiting unearned feelings of superiority. Such characters illustrated their pretension by boasting, ignoring their neighbors, or treating them with disrespect.

In "*Di feder*" (The Pen), a group of office implements—an eraser, a pencil, a lighter, a penknife, a three-hole punch, a leather notebook, a pair of scissors, and a pen in an inkwell—are left behind in an office at the end of a workday. All the implements converse except for the pen. She (Yiddish is a gendered language) doesn't want to speak with the common folk. The pen, who writes in a highly ornamental style, whose words are like pearls and whose talent is famous around the world, doesn't believe that she should have to converse with just anyone. The implements fall silent out of shame. Only the leather covered book directs a few words to the wall: "Such a gigantic talent, in such a small container . . ."

The poem asserts that a talent can be enormous, but the person manifesting such a talent is diminished in stature when (s)he displays snobbish and self-aggrandizing behavior.

In "*A Golden-pen*" (A Golden Pen), the writer explains what makes one big or small even more clearly. This fable is written from the perspective of an observer who asks whether it is an illness or a passion that the golden pen is haughty and looks down on everyone. He wonders if she thinks it is below her to greet her neighbors, because she believes that she is crowned with God-given talent. The writer acknowledges that the golden pen has a mighty talent, is industrious, and her essence is as deep as aged wine in a casket. He asks why a giant needs to be bigger than she already is. It is modesty and generosity, per the fabulist, that makes one greater and deserving of an ornamental crown.

I wondered, reading this fable, whether the impetus for exploring this theme lay in my father's post-war relationships with other Yiddish writers or whether its roots lay deep in his earlier life in Vilna. My father struggled to express vulnerability in personal relationships. The fable form gave him the tools to address his observations pointedly and I suspected that some of his personal injuries were expressed through these animated objects.

Boastfulness and pretention were a frequent theme in my father's poetry. He clearly observed it in others, but I also wondered how much consciousness he had about his own habit of boasting and whether it arose out of feelings of insecurity, which may have originated in his own familial relationships and/or in his experiences as an immigrant.

Reading through my father's books, I always felt relieved when I came to the fable section. Many of the fables have serious themes, but they are wrapped in humor and whimsy. A rare fable contains solely humor and whimsy, without a moral center, critique, or wisdom to impart. This fable, translated by my sister Libi, entitled "*Reklames*" (Advertising), retains much of the playfulness of the original Yiddish version.

In a little village, in a wire pen,
lived a downy duck, and a yellow hen
One evening they met when out for a walk
and with a quack and cluck began to talk.
After discussing the news of the day,
the duck asked the chicken in her timid way:

"Chicken, you know I admire you greatly.
I have a problem I've been pondering lately
that I'd very much like to ask you about.
You could answer it chicken, of that I've no doubt."

Said the hen to the duck: "Go ahead, ask away."
So the duck heaved a sigh and said "Answer this, pray."

Why is it that your eggs are so easy to sell,
scrambled or boiled, in or out of the shell?
Everyone buys them, but much to my shame,
though my eggs are larger, and taste just the same,
they're left where they are, people just pass them by.
What's wrong with them hen? Can you tell me why?"

The hen frowned and said: "Answer this, try this tack."
"When you sit down to lay, do you cluck? Do you quack?"
"Why no," said the duck, "I sit still as a nun
and quietly strain 'til my labour is done."
"And after you've laid, do you cackle or shout?"
"I just rise," said the duck, "and go silently out."

"What a fool," cried the hen, that chicken so sly.
"You stay mute, you're silent, and you wonder why?
When I settle down, there's no one can doubt it.
When I start to lay, all the world knows about it.
Before I begin, I make sure that I'm heard,
and when I am done, everyone's got the word."

"If your eggs don't sell, then I strongly advise
make a noise, let them know. Go ahead, advertise."

It occurred to me after reading *"Reklames"* that my father must have been ongoingly and increasingly concerned about readership for his books, so that "advertising" was not merely a playful theme but perhaps a provocative idea. A poem in *A zemer fun demer* (A Song from the Twilight), his last book, laments that even friends are no longer buying his books.

My sister Libi, the translator of this fable, left home at the age of seventeen for a year's work and study on a kibbutz. She remained in Israel to complete her BA at The Hebrew University of Jerusalem. She remembers translating this poem at the age of twenty-three when she returned to Toronto after my mother's death. My father had given her several poems and fables that he wanted translated into English, and she chose this one because she found it amusing. She remembered that he was not pleased with the translation. He was very critical of her use of words that weren't in the original fable as well as the imperfectly matching meters in several lines. She told me that this was the end of her translation efforts.

My father never asked me to translate any of his poems, although he did show me some of his own English translations of his Yiddish poetry and ask me for my opinion. I regret that I was as dismissive of his efforts as he was of my sister's. I don't know what he would think of my English translations of his poetry, although I suspect that his striving for perfection of rhyme and meter would make my translations unsatisfactory to him. I'm sorry that we never had the conversation about the difficulties of translating from one language to another.

A vehicle for humor and whimsy, fables were also a vehicle in which my father could express the deep spiritual struggles that accompanied his life's mission to keep the Yiddish language and culture alive, to keep going and writing even as his readership diminished by the year.

The fable "*A moshl mit a froshl*" (A Fable with a Frog), published in his book of fables *Tvishn shmeykhl un troyer* (Between Smile and Tear), has the same folksy, humorous tone as does "*Reklames*," but offers a message about the value of continually striving in the face of adversity.

In "*A moshl mit a proshl*," my father first sets the scene, as he does in many of his fables. Two cows, one red, one yellow, are milked by Stella in the morning. She leaves the half pailful of milk to cool in the shade of a shed. A frog jumps into the fable from a nearby spring and hops into the pail of milk. But the frog is not worried, as frogs are good swimmers. He swims for an hour, then two, before the strain shows. His back hurts and he is getting tired, but he struggles to go on, even though the milk is getting thicker. It is hard to see how this will end well for the frog. And yet, when he can barely swim another round, his foot taps something solid. His perseverance in continuing to swim despite the negative odds of surviving created an island of butter. And this butter island that the frog created rescues him from drowning in the milk. The writer states at the end that the moral (which is typically outlined with a clear pithy statement at the end of a fable) is left for readers to discover for themselves.

I love this fable for its optimism. It's one of my favorites of my father's works. I accepted his invitation to discover the moral for myself. In my view, consciously or not, my father owned and admired perseverance and fighting for life until one's last bit of strength ebbed. And to translate from frog into human terms, in so doing, he created an "island," a place of refuge where he could stand despite hardship, despite his unfamiliar, indifferent, and often hostile environment. He did this by remaining faithful to his language and his craft. One can drown in sorrow, or one can create a refuge by continuing to swim.

In "*Roykh un pare*" (Smoke and Steam), the fable centers on an encounter between a wisp of smoke and a cloud. As wanderers do in unfamiliar environments, they greet one another and begin to ask about one another's origins and destinations. The cloud asks the smoke what enclosure he has climbed out from. The smoke replies that he was bored with fires and kitchens, smelters and brick enclosures. He has just escaped from prison through the chimney. He is climbing up "to the infinite." He will "gather stars like gold coins" and wander with winds from one place to another. He has earned his due and is seeking comfort and rest.

The smoke asks the cloud where it is floating to. "The highest forgiveness," says the cloud. "I've wandered, pregnant with snow and hail long enough. I'm longing for the earth, for the dark ground, for sunny, fertile fields. I want to pour out my heart in the rain and fall to the earth and on everything that spreads out nearby. I want to unite with hot sands and piles of stones and green the flats and the hills. And understand an old expression: A cloud that falls from the heights to its last drop, on sands and on bare stones is a pilgrim. And a wisp of smoke that climbs to the heavens unhappy, a rebel, is an expatriate."

I read this fable, as I did so many, as a disguised manifesto about my father's spiritual mission. This fable expresses his belief in what he intended to do and would continue to do until he died. He, as the cloud/poet, was a wanderer away from home who had been carrying the burden of hail and snow for a long time. As the cloud/poet, in his last days, he wanted to fall to the earth, emptying his heart to the last drop. And even as he knew that the last drops of rain might fall on barren sand and stone, the effort alone, the continued adherence to his holy mission, made him a pilgrim as compared to one who tried to escape the conditions of his life, who was merely an expatriate.

The rhyme and rhythm of these fables when read in their original Yiddish provide the aesthetic pleasure of sound and meter not available in English translation. They also function, as noted earlier, to deepen one's understanding of what is being written.

By now, I had learned that my father was a modernist poet/ fabulist. He placed himself squarely in the modernist tradition of Yiddish poetry by varying the length of lines and stanzas, by rhyming Yiddish words with words that originate in *loshn khoydish* (the holy language, Hebrew), by rhyming two words with one, and by creating neologisms. In so doing, my father and *Yung-Vilne* were creating new forms of Yiddish expression.

My father's poems are rich in Hebrew-Aramaic expressions, more so when he is emphasizing spiritual themes. The words chosen to describe the cloud and the smoke describe a person's relationship with Israel, the Holy Land. The cloud is an *oyle* (pilgrim), one who goes "up" to seek spiritual attainment and fulfilment. The same word is used for those who move to dwell in Israel and those who go to the lectern to read the Torah. The smoke is a *yoyred*, a word used for anyone who leaves Israel, and also translates as an impoverished or ruined person.

It is a holy act to remember, carry, and write about what has been lost, even when there are no ears to hear. It is a holy act to continue this mission until one's very last breath. I was impressed that my father wanted to end his days empty of words, fully expressed.

The perfidy of the Soviet Union preaching a classless society while creating a police state was a theme in my father's writing up until and including his last book, which was published in 1991. The book *Tvishn shmeykhl un trer* (Between Smile and Tear), published in 1979 and composed only of fables, contains eight that can be described as political as they deal with themes of poverty and injustice, or the role of "mediators" and "collaborators," or the denial of responsibility for political crimes. Sometimes the finger is pointed squarely at Russia, as in a fable about a "red" rope that calls a guillotine a "murderer" for cutting off heads while denying its own crimes. (It merely "chokes").

In the fable "*A tzadik in pelts*" (A Saint in Fur), sheep no longer want to be sacrificed as food for their killers. They are sick of being served boiled or roasted, so they gather together in great numbers, learn to be tough, and teach a harsh lesson to the hyenas and wolves who hunt them, by pounding them with their hooves, punishing and slaughtering them. The hyenas and wolves howl out "help" in their shock and fear. A "red" bear lives in the forest. This "prince of justice" believes himself to be generous to the other animals in the forest because he is, after all, their lord.

But in the shadows of trees, where he can't be seen, he slings back sheep gravy, which, the poet remarks in an aside, is not exactly reducing his girth. He rants that he is the red bear who releases the world from injustice and provides for his subjects with his own hide. He begins to roar and goes to the wolves' rescue. He will release them from murderers and robbers and hangmen and make of these interlopers a pile of rubble. He sends pilgrims with sharp teeth and fangs to the rescue and soon his flag is smeared red with the world's blood. And in the woods, animals applaud him, calling him the "the righteous one in fur."

This fable reveals my father's skills and originality in Yiddish. "*A Tzadik in pelts*" translates literally as a saint or righteous person in fur, but it refers idiomatically in Yiddish to a rabbi who goes around well dressed.

My father unpacks the metaphor of the righteous person in fur and brings it to life. There is something suspicious about a well-turned-out rabbi, according to my father. The "red" bear signals unmistakeably that he was writing about the Soviet Union. I read this fable in the first months of the Russian war with Ukraine in the spring of 2022, and the self-righteousness, self-justification, and duplicity expressed in this fable echoed decades later.

Unlike his earliest political critiques, which needed to be subtly disguised, the characters in several fables in his last book point explicitly to the Soviet Union. In *"Ber un odler"* (Bear and Eagle), Ivan the Bear is a schoolmaster and teaches his students with anger and without compassion, with sharp teeth and a knotty pointer. If his students fail to learn, they are sent to remedial school in Siberia.

Considering the fable form, there is sometimes surprising depth found within my father's political vision, a broad overview which gives a concrete situation a humane, philosophical perspective rather than resorting to simple "us and them" moralizing. For example, in *"Beymer"* (Trees), a birch grove with white stems complains that a fir tree ("a pitch and tar tree") that has come to dwell in its midst doesn't belong there. The fir tree protests, asking if he is supposed to tear his roots out of the earth. Yet the birch grove curses the fir tree: "May a storm uproot it." The curse works. A storm brings lightning and strong winds that burn the entire forest.

This fable says that the consequences of hatred are not limited to the intended victims. And, as I learned more and more through his works, the fable is not a simple entertainment for children. It is a legitimate art form in which profound themes are discussed.

A fable entitled *"A kaktusl"* (A Little Cactus) surprised me with its compassionate and hopeful message. Someone has bought a cactus and planted it in a garden. But the cactus, a child of "desert hell," is covered with spiny thorns. One cannot approach it without feeling its piercing anger. How can such a plant be tolerated in the garden? An aster takes it upon herself to complain to the owner of the garden. The owner hears her out and then reprimands her. The aster doesn't know that the poor cactus was wrenched out of the desert sand. The cactus lived through whirlwinds and hot sand and thirst and conflagration. One must have spiny weapons to protect oneself in such circumstances. The landholder explains that everything needs time. When the cactus has lived among the other plants, in time it will stop being afraid of friends and neighbors. The fable ends with these four lines:

> And just as time has wrenched him
> from a country dead and dark,
> time will also wrench
> the thistles from his heart.

Was my father knowingly writing about himself as the cactus with the spiny thorns developed in a hostile, foreign land still needed to protect himself? I hope so, as his closing message is optimistic, compassionate, and self-forgiving.

Reading through my father's books allowed me to see how he developed the fable form and made it his own. My father's early fables were strongly influenced by Eliezer Shteynbarg. But as he continued to write, he developed this form into one that was uniquely his.

In a recorded talk my father gave at the Jewish Public Library in Montreal on the occasion of his second book being published in 1974 (available on the Yiddish Book Center website[2]), he said that sometimes his poems could start with the intention of being a poem and then become a fable, and vice versa. In later fables, some of the traditional elements of the fable remained, but some were relinquished altogether.

"*Nit derzogt*" (Incompletely Expressed), for which my father received the Manger Prize, is the only one of my father's books containing only lyric poetry with no fable section. Yet several poems in this book seem to have drawn from aspects of the fable. The poem "*Zun yam vint*" (Sun, Sea, Wind) takes place in a natural setting, in which the elements have genders, personalities, and desires.

2. https://www.yiddishbookcenter.org.

Yiddish is a gendered language. Each tree, bird, drop of rain, and ray of sun has a gender, masculine, feminine, or neuter. This feature of the language lends itself to characterization. So, for example, in this poem the sun is feminine, and the rays of the sun are the strands of her hair. It reads:

> The sun buttons up her nightgown—a cloud,
> a silver nightgown with crimson buttons,
> and dips her golden strands
> into the sea's depths.

> The sea, turbulent to its black abyss,
> starts to dazzle with various colours.
> He still carries the reflection of the sun in his heart,
> even when the storm wind starts to stir him up

> The wind, his old intimate buddy
> is also in love with the sun's blondness.
> He begrudges the sun her blonde shimmer
> when she bathes in the sea's depths.

> She loosens her gold blond locks
> into the heart of the sea and flirts with him . . .
> The sea starts to flame pink in the morning
> with green emeralds and blue sapphires.

> The wind becomes a wild tempest with jealousy.
> He throws himself on the sea with a fearful tempest.
> He wants to bedeck the naked incandescent sun
> with grey clouds to cover her body.

> But the sea does not allow this, he defies the wind,
> even though he's a friend, love is stronger.
> He hurls his waves angrily in this fight
> and swirls and hits the wind, the interloper, violently.

But the wind still flies around on whirling wings.
He tears pieces from the sea, to discredit the sun.
He has already broken the sea into pieces
to keep the sun from showing her face there.

The sun, hidden, peeks out from a crack
and smiles to herself about the whole story.
Down there two foolish males are fighting.
They think they are the sun's paramours.

Tomorrow they'll let go of their anger.
The sea and the wind will stop their noise
and in the rosy early morning,
she will come again to wash her golden hair in the sea.

In this poem, the elements are developed to create a complete short story full of wry observations about love, friendship, and jealousy, while affirming the power of female choice. It is an example of a poem that may have started out as a fable.

The very first fable in my father's last book, *A Zemer fun demer* (A Song from the Twilight), published in 1991 when he was eighty-three years old, is entitled "*Tzvey brider*" (Two Brothers). At this point in my father's development of the fable form, the two protagonists are neither animals nor plants nor implements, and the fable is not set in the natural world. They are instead two aspects of my father's personality.

In this fable-poem, my father speaks of having two distinct souls—twins—in his one body. One is an old man, whose hair is greying, whose face is carved with deep lines. The second is a young man, whose green eyes still sparkle. The old man judges, counts his days, and focuses on his mistakes. The young man still breathes with life and has thoughts that he wants to share. They are twins in one body. A couplet closes the poem: "One writes lonely poems, the other cheerful fables."

My father had green eyes, a startling and unusual shade of green. He had black hair, which thinned and greyed but still kept some of its black into old age. He was a short man, who kvelled over my brother's greater height. He was slim in my early memories and stocky and muscular in his later years. He had a strong, chiseled face, which could look stern in repose but could break into a wide grin and laugh that lit up his face. He spoke about having been a ruffian in his youth. He loved practical jokes; he loved to play; he loved women. He was lusty and alive, not averse to telling an off-color joke.

The young soul was the fun-loving father who often appeared when small children were around, who liked to do magic tricks for them, to pretend to swallow coins and make them appear from behind their ears. In summer months at a rented cottage, he organized children into teams and fashioned treasure hunt quests composed of rhyming couplets leading us from clue to clue.

I also remember the judgmental soul, who could be brutal in his criticism, particularly of other people's writing. In addition to the anecdote mentioned earlier about my sister Libi translating the fable "*Reklames*" (Advertising), Libi also told me a story of a poem she wrote in English when she was eleven, at my father's request. She still remembers the poem and the stern look on his face as he said, "This is not a poem."

I did not know until I read my father's poetry that the victim of his severest judgments was he himself.

I read "*Tzvey brider*" (Two Brothers) very early in my poem-a-day practice. It was instructive and carried me through all the books of poetry and fables I read. It brought me comfort to think about my father's young, living soul when I entered into his darker world.

A fable in his last book titled "*A shturem*" (A Storm) made enough of an impression on me that I translated it trying to retain the rhythm and rhyme of the original Yiddish, as follows:

> A violent wind came rushing down
> into a world that bloomed and pleased
> and whipped the water into foam
> and ripped the beards from flowering trees.

It turned the houses upside down;
left broken doors and shattered beams.
The damage done, at dusk it left
a shtetl smashed to smithereens.

At night the stars came out to write
a message with a silver pen:
that everything that was destroyed
would grow in beauty once again.

For in the people as in trees
in everything that grows and greens
lies a great mysterious power
stronger than the might of winds.

The sun in dawn's caressing light
washed the golden earth with dew
surprising that accursed storm
with the life it would renew.

It lifted up the trampled grass
and comforted the trembling folk,
redeeming what the storm had wrought,
making whole what hatred broke.

For in their souls are people blessed
both with their dreams and with their faith
and all that is destroyed by storms
is lifted up another day.

My father writes that people have two sources to turn to when their lives are shattered, and they need inspiration to go on. One is religious faith, and the other is a dream, a mission. Despite all the losses and the terrible, ongoing grief, my father contained within himself a great, mysterious power, a mission that elevated him and allowed him to go on and continue to create. My father's dream came up over and over in his writing. He never spelled out directly what his dream was, although it became clearer the more I read and the more I understood.

Chapter 4: Creation

In the course of reading, I grew fascinated by the poems that describe my father's creative process. These are the poems I love the most; they seem to stem from a source that was so much stronger and more available to him than anything I have ever experienced in my own writing.

My father's urge to write was always evident in our home. In every room—the kitchen, living room, bedroom—and on every surface—the backs of envelopes and bills, the blank sides of letter inserts—there were scribbled lines of Yiddish, thoughts that needed to be captured immediately and words and phrases that would hopefully end up as poems and fables.

I saw this, but before reading through my father's books, I didn't understand how compelled he was to write, how this was his calling, how something inside could rise up and require words to give expression to his deepest feelings and inspiration. He himself was awed by what happened to him. Without his conscious will, he would become entranced by something in nature, for example, and then words would appear and flow from the source. He had a mystic connection to his muse. He described this process over and over again. Here it is in *"Regnboygns"* (Rainbows).

The sun slices off the tops of dark clouds

with a golden saw.

A golden rain shimmers

accompanying my steps.

A melody, a rare melody
sings within me like a flute
and my heart begins to sway with joy
upon illuminated musical strings.

I walk, musing, a listener
and in my depths
sparkling Yiddish words ring out
and lay themselves out in a poem.

My loneliness ebbs,
my joy flickers like a candle.
Such, such simple beauty—
is hard to translate into words.

I walk teary-eyed, a detective,
in the golden spray of the rain.
I am looking for words for the raindrops
and they do not reveal their names.

In every book of poetry, organized under various chapter headings, there is a section devoted to this experience of inspiration and creation. I found my father's spirituality there, his belief system, and his understanding of God. These are poems I could not have appreciated in my younger adulthood, when I was more oriented to worldly concerns, but I resonated with them now as I read through his works.

My father was deeply inspired to write by what he found in nature, but also by what he discovered within himself. When he was stirred, something magical seemed to happen to him, especially, as he told his readers, when the sun went down. He wrote about being filled with Yiddish words, with rhymes that seemed to come to him from some unearthly place, from his ancestors, from a hidden holy man, or from God. This marriage of the deep imperative to write and the Yiddish words that seemed to flow from a source outside of him was welcomed by him with joy and gratitude, especially after an absence.

If asked, my father probably would have said he didn't believe in God. I remember him saying he couldn't believe in God after the Holocaust. In his words around the dinner table, my father often expressed antipathy not toward religious orthodoxy itself, but toward religious hypocrisy, toward those who claimed a particular relationship to God through their dress and ritualistic behavior, but who behaved in unscrupulous ways. As a Yiddishist, he would have taken a critical stance toward some religious practices. My family did not attend synagogue and the one and only time I saw the inside of one as a child was when my mother took her children to hear the shofar blown on Rosh Hashanah.

Even though my father did not believe in God as a fundamental and active agent in the world, he talked to God often in his poetry as a way of addressing and protesting the world as it was, in line with the Jewish practice of talking and debating directly with God. "God" was a word he used, although not the only one, for the source of all creation. My father experienced this source as mystical and deeply sustaining. From this perspective, God could appear as the essence of a flower or the deepest truth in a person's heart.

But when my father was remembering his losses, God could appear as a manipulator or as unconcerned about the pain of human beings. Similarly, in God's relationship to the natural world, in one poem God could appear as a being who observed the natural world and so admired its beauty that he would trade it for heaven. And in another poem, when my father was thinking about war and destruction, he described God as weeping at what people have done to the world.

God had yet other incarnations in my father's poetry. In "*A Lidele vigt zikh*" (A Poem Rocks Itself), my father speaks about a mysterious "other" who visits him at nightfall and transforms him into a viola with golden strings upon which the other then plays his tune. The poem is thus a co-creation; the other is disembodied and needs my father's words and lips with which to create poetry.

The magical other is also the inspiration, the one that haunts his dreams and sows the kernels of poems within him.

In *"Verter vos shprotzn"* (Words that Sprout), he asks who has sown this abundance of words within him and answers that these words are the echoes of ancient ancestors. He is their heir, in whom their words mature. The "other," it seems, was at times a playful partner, and at times the weighty words of disembodied past generations.

In other poems, God was also his deepest truth and the conscience that spoke to him about how he needed to elevate himself. He also said that the version of God who dwelled in heaven was a construct made up by people both in the past and in the present. The God that existed for him dwells here among us, in our consciences, in our desire to be and do good.

My father was not alone among creative people in experiencing the creative impulse as both stemming from within and also as a necessary and vital partnership. He seemed so utterly in love with this mysterious process and so blessed with the fruits of that relationship, richly rewarded with an abundance of words that clamored to become poems.

In the poem *"Grine verter"* (Green Words), the poet describes himself as having lost his way on a summer's evening, walking through the disorder of the city and finding himself in a green meadow. He has been illuminated as if by a lantern as he walks, and he hears his green words mature within him. He writes that nobody knows that behind his eyes lives another being who illuminates all his darkness and accompanies his bare essence. This being tills his depths and sows seeds within them, skimmed from his past and from his dreams. That is why from within poems both dreamed and inherited sprout in him "bloody and red as cherries." He hears a sparrow sing and knows that it is his own melody it is whistling. A delicious ear of corn sways in the wind, and he knows it is his own murmur echoing, as his depths are being plowed by a hidden holy man.

He experiences a profound wholeness and connectedness with nature. The outside and inside are one. This experience of oneness, merging with one's environment, is a mystical experience described in many spiritual traditions.

"*S'treft*" (It Happens) is a short poem in which my father reveals the power of the creative process within him:

A single word begins just with light:
The bluest hours awaken in me,
my body becomes a cello
with shivering, trembling strings.
And something takes me by the throat
and shakes me with such force
that drops of blood and teardrops
mingle together inside me.
And everything becomes like the essence of poppies
and intoxicates my senses—

And my thoughts like my garments
become clothed in melody and words.

Each one of these poems about the creative process moves me. My father lost everything, but not this connection to his Creator, who spoke to him in his own language and demanded, in a manner he experienced viscerally, that he continue to craft his Yiddish poetry. Despite the sadness in so much of his poetry, it seems that it was this power—his godly power that never deserted him—that allowed him to conquer his despair and continue his work.

The poet realized that what began with inspiration needed to be shaped and crafted. He spoke about this in the recorded talk he gave in 1974 (mentioned in chapter 3) during an evening convened at the Jewish Public Library of Montreal. This night celebrated the release of his second book, *Shures shire* (Lines of Song), twenty-three years after his first book, *A Likht far a groshn*, was published. He spoke about having written constantly in the twenty-three intervening years since his first book was published, but without the confidence that the material was strong enough for a book. Why he finally decided to put this book out was a bit of a mystery to him, he said, but perhaps it was so that his frozen tears could begin to flow and make room for more and different kinds of poems and fables.

He said that a good writer is not one who can write, but one who can erase over and over again. He emphasized that a writer needs the courage to see his own mistakes. Just as when in draining a cup of sour cream, something is always left on the sides of a cup, he felt that some of the meaning of a poem always remains in the arteries of the heart.

I was struck by how poetic and articulate he was in his own language, compared to his lifelong struggles with English. I recognized and appreciated, yet again, how frustrating and humiliating it must have been to live in a country in which life was negotiated in a language that he was never comfortable in, so that he could never truly be seen and understood amongst people who didn't speak Yiddish, including family members on my mother's side and his own children.

My father wrote poems that spoke about who he was as a poet, how poems were created within him, what his poetic aspirations were, and, inevitably, how the Holocaust shaped his poetic themes.

In "*A Lid tsu zikh*" (A Poem to Myself), the poet speaks to himself about what a poem must be. It is his writing credo. This poem reveals his deep intention and hope for all the writing he sent out into the world. He believes that his poetry should have ideals, so that ideals might become reality. He wants his poetry and fables to be as polished and clear as a spring. Every word has to be a truth gained from living, nurtured in his own being, so that others can hear their own pain reflected, so that they can be inspired by his own aspiration to find their own desires. My father writes that poems should not be overtly didactic or programmatic, or contain obscure symbolism. His poems need to resonate in someone else to have value.

In another poem, also called "*Tsu zikh*" (To Myself), he speaks to himself about how to approach the process of writing a poem. He tells himself to wait before providing a response, to seek his depths, to polish and sharpen his words. "All the yet unfound melodies wait in the strings of a harp . . . All the fodder of language and incantation are saved up, hidden in the rooms of the body." He will need all of these words when the time comes, full of tension, "like a bud ready to burst into bloom." And from his treasure trove, through his pores, words will arise. This treasure contains old words from his grandmother, and young words from his own core, when his longing and his sharp grief combine to find expression in a poem.[1]

Yet there is a tension in this poem. He is a "mute harp" that songs embrace. Although a melody is already fluttering in his heart, his stubborn lips are still silent, not yet ready. He must wait, yet he asks himself how many hours he has left, and tells himself to hurry, that tomorrow is too late. Young, sparkling songs are waiting in his depths, and demanding *tikkun* (healing, salvation of the soul).

This tension between his inner drive to create, his own writing creed (which demanded perfect alignment with his muse), and his awareness of the limited time still available to him was a theme that grew in urgency from book to book.

My father wrote many poems about the burden and contradiction of his destiny as a poet, who was compelled to write yet was writing in a dying language, for readers of Yiddish works were diminishing by the year.

When our small family arrived in Montreal in 1949 as immigrants, my father made his living by working in a warehouse as a cleaner and a shipper. In 1955, he was hired by the *Tog-morgn zhurnal* (Day-Morning Journal), a Yiddish daily newspaper based in New York, as a subscription manager. His job required him to travel to cities in eastern Ontario and New York state to collect payment from subscribers and renew their subscriptions. Circulation

1. In this stanza, when the poet speaks of carrying old words from his grandmother's treasure and new ones from his own center, he illustrates this point and underlines his modernity as a poet by rhyming an old word with a newly created one. *Oyster* is the word for treasure, and *Bloy-tser*, meaning blue grief, is a neologism, a newly created word.

of the *Tog-morgn zhurnal* was estimated at fifty thousand in 1970 and the newspaper stopped publishing in 1971.

After the *Tog* ceased publication, my father began doing similar work for another Yiddish daily, the *Forverts*, but by 1983 it was being published only once a week. The newspapers would then arrive in Toronto weekly from New York by Greyhound bus. As we didn't own a car, my father arranged for someone to pick up the newspapers at the bus terminal and drive them to the corner stores that still sold Yiddish newspapers.

My father travelled for the *Tog* about once a month, for approximately ten days at a time. During these trips, my father would have become acutely aware of the diminishing readership of Yiddish newspapers as readers died and fewer subscriptions were renewed. In his daily work, he saw up close the dying of a language and with it the culture it contained. In 1990, the year before my father's last book was published and three years before his death, the *Forverts* Yiddish weekly had a circulation of only seven thousand people.

The grim reality of this decline in Yiddish readership is reflected in a poem entitled "*A dank*" (Thank You). In it, my father gives thanks for his poetic soul, which he likens to having a "seven-colored rainbow" hung in his eyes, the "unrest of a tempest" trickled into his blood, and a dream "fashioned from a sliver of a falling star." Turning to his present reality and his ongoing dilemma of writing in a dying language, he writes that he is lonely in the city, lit up and noisy, as disappointed as a wanderer in a desert who has found his long-sought well dried out.

His mother language is still on his lips and he loops together words like pearls on a chain even though he knows his "musical band," his musician companions, will not be returning. In a poignant verse, he wonders if it is his destiny to wander around "on tiptoes," seeking a young heir who will inherit his melody. But he finds only grey heads and eyes with their light extinguished even as his language demands expression. Even though he knows that death will come and extinguish his melody, he continues to move to its rhythm. "The white baby goat" of his rhymes continues to baa behind him with a thousand offerings.[2]

Then, he points the reader to something he has just done in the previous verse. He tells us that he writes with allusions and symbols that point to the old and holy times. Even though his temples are grey, he still remembers the songs he heard as a little boy.

He wonders for whom is he sharing these intimate words and who in these noisy streets can hear his voice. His last days are becoming sad, tired, and filled with longing. It becomes harder the older he gets to fool himself with young, believing words, even though his inspiration still fills him with light. He closes this powerful poem with two lines describing what remains within him.

> words, half forgotten that demand their due
> and faces, that I can already not identify.

Although the creative impulse was strong and compelling in my father, the following poem let me know that he had fallow times as well, and that even his creative times in Canada did not compare to how it was when everything in his world was Yiddish. "*Ikh benk*" (I Yearn), is a strong poem that held surprises for me. The poem begins, "The older I get, the more I yearn . . ."

He yearns for his former dream, which once flew to the skies but now can only crawl on the earth. He says that he left a friend behind—hunger—"that which has wings." He describes himself now as being full, with a fullness that hangs around his belly, and roots him to the earth, so that the heaviness in his body does not allow his dream which wants to fly, to lift off. The older he gets, the more everything draws him back, to everything he holds dear, where his father "woke the day" with songs and prayers, where everything was Yiddish, where Yiddish was spoken by his

---

2. See "Why a Goat," https://www.yiddishbookcenter.org/about/why-goat. The Yiddish song "*Rozhinkes mit mandlen*" (Raisins and Almonds) tells of a goat asleep under a baby's cradle. Goats appear in Chagall's paintings, and in poems and stories by many Yiddish writers including Mendele, Peretz, Sholem Aleichem, Kadia Molodiwsky, Avrom Sutzkever, Chaim Grade, and Isaac Bashevis Singer.

Christian neighbors, where his generation blossomed. He closes with an image of himself trapped in a cage, in a country that worships the golden calf.

Here again is the contrast between spiritual and poetic flourishing versus alienation. Elsewhere, he applied the theme of hunger as the impetus for creative expression to other writers.

I was surprised to find him apply this idea to his own creative expression. I wondered if he meant the physical hunger that comes from poverty, or the hunger for change, for justice and for equality, which animated so many of his generation of writers in Eastern Europe. I did not know until I read it in this poem that my father's Christian neighbors spoke Yiddish.

This tension between the inner demand to write and the dying of the language in which my father wrote accompanied him his entire life. My father wrote poems until the very end, even during the many hospitalizations for his failing heart. In an article written about him on the first anniversary of his death, Moshe Wolf quoted a final poem that he wrote several weeks before his death:[3]

> I shall ignite a fire on this last piece of paper.
> May it burn for a few minutes, if it has nothing to say.
> It is becoming dark and darker.
> I've nothing more to give.
> A little light, a little shine for my heart;
> Here, take it all away,
> my last bit of love—to the very end!
> It is just with this that I will remain.
> in the dark end.

3. I am grateful to Moshe Wolf for providing me with this unpublished article.

Chapter 5: Family

Like other families headed by Holocaust survivors, the extended family I knew was small and widely scattered. Only one of my father's six siblings survived the Holocaust, and one of my mother's two siblings survived. My father's parents had both died natural deaths before the war; my mother's parents were murdered.

A few cousins survived and lived in New York, Finland, and Mexico. Family visits were rare and reserved for special occasions. My father's surviving sister, Etke, lived in Montreal. She lost a husband and child in the Holocaust and never remarried. There were no discussions in my family about which relatives had whose features or talents, no discussions about who resembled whom. Neither of my parents spoke about the people they had loved and lost. There are many things I discovered about my father's inner world through his poetry and fables, but unexpectedly, reading his poetry, I discovered isolated facts that I never knew about certain family members. Each of those poems incidentally described physical and personality traits of my father's family members. In them, I found similarities in my generation and in the one following mine.

My father wrote a few poems that relayed events from his life that were both amusing and made a lasting impression. Very early in my reading, I encountered a poem about one of his sister's children, a boy whose name was Leyzerl. He called this poem "*Leyzerl, an emese mayse*" (Leyzerl, a True Story). This story is a rhymed recollection of an event from my father's young adulthood in Vilna.

I learned from the poem that his nephew, the eight-year-old son of his sister Basya-Mindl, was a mischievous little boy, always in trouble. Basya-Mindl and her family lived in a cottage next door to their parents. My father was living with his parents in their cottage at the time. Leyzerl's father was a pedlar, a traveling salesman, who came home only for Shabbos. My father was asked by his sister to discipline the boy for some trouble he had gotten into. What he decided to do was to convene a jury of the boy's peers who decided together that Leyzerl's punishment should be prison in a chicken coop jail. Leyzerl, to my father's delight, responded, "Fine, I'll go into the chicken coop, but I'm not laying any eggs."

Reading this poem, which I remember my father telling as an amusing anecdote, I realized as if for the first time that among my father's losses and mine was a young first cousin. I had known about the murdered uncle, aunts, and one cousin (a daughter of my aunt Etke) on my father's side and the murdered grandparents, uncles, aunts, and cousins on my mother's side, but Leyzerl had just been a child in an amusing anecdote my father told before I read this detailed poem.

The central story my father told us about what happened to his family during the Holocaust was that of several of his siblings and a cousin hiding in a bunker in the forest outside the Vilna ghetto. Their location was betrayed by a farmer and a grenade was thrown into the bunker by the Nazis when they (all but one cousin who survived to tell the story) refused the order to come out. Leyzerl was never mentioned. Was he in the bunker or had he been taken earlier in a ghetto action? What was his father's name? I never asked these questions when I could, and my father never volunteered the information. I thought about my nephew Zael, who was also lively and full of mischief s as a child. My father adored Zael. Did Zael remind him of Leyzerl? He never said.

A long poem, "*A boym afn dakh*" (A Tree on the Roof) is another of my father's family anecdotes, but this is a story I never heard him tell. In this poem, my father describes how a wild pear tree took root in his family's yard, but produced only hard, sour pears, which "we" (I assume his family and friends) ate and suffered the stomach aches that followed.

His father, whom he describes here as a "dreamer and idealist about all sorts of things," decided a real fruit-bearing tree could be grafted onto this wild pear tree. He asked Vasili, an orchard keeper and neighbor, for help. Vasili sawed all the branches from the wild pear tree and grafted twigs from a fruit-bearing pear tree on it. All the cuts were wrapped in flax and lime was smeared on the wrapped twigs.

Three years later, the tree bloomed and by the end of that summer, the tree was laden with giant yellow, red-cheeked pears. After a couple of years, my father's father wanted to build a shed for their wood-carrying wagon in the yard. This would have meant cutting down the pear tree, but cutting down a fruit-bearing tree is forbidden in the Torah. So, my father's devout father allowed the tree to remain in the middle of the yard and built a stable with a roof on it around the tree. And so, a pear tree grew on the roof. My father's friends didn't believe him . . .

> until I invited my friends to our place
> and showed them I wasn't joking.
> At our house a pear tree grew on the roof
> bedecked with yellow, red-cheeked pears.

I didn't know my father's father was a dreamer and idealist, I didn't know the Torah forbids the cutting down of a fruit-bearing tree, and I didn't know my father's house had a pear tree on the roof of its shed. I assume that Vasili was one of the gentile neighbors on the street who spoke Yiddish, which, as I mentioned earlier, I only learned while reading my father's poetry.

In the poem "*Mayn zeyde*" (My Grandfather), my father describes how his grandfather Yakov Shloyme resisted all attempts by his sons and daughters to give up his own modest cottage and come to live with them.

Yakov would rise early in the morning and go out to the streets to find the neediest members of the community, whether they be poor, lame, or drunk. He would convince them to come with him to his cottage, where he would give them his bed, cook for them, wash them, and trim their elflocks. Because of this behavior, my father's grandfather was the subject of the community's mockery; his home was jokingly called the "poorhouse" or the "almshouse."

Yakov's children, including my grandfather Avrom, were scandalized by this behavior and begged their father to come live in one of their homes, which he refused to do. In response to the family's entreaties, he would ask what was the point of life if not to do good deeds.

I learned from this poem not only about the goodness of my great-grandfather, but about the hierarchical and snobbish nature of the Jewish community, where outward signs of prosperity and success were admired while examples of profound piety were mocked or unvalued. My father elaborated on this theme over and over in his fables.

A poem entitled "*Mayn tate un mayn zayde*" (My Father and my Grandfather) describes an amusing source of tension between the poet's father and grandfather. As in the previous poem, my grandfather Avrom was described as an influential man who associated with those whom he found suitable—this in contrast to my great-grandfather Yakov, who befriended the ordinary people on the street. What's more, my grandfather was blond and my great-grandfather had very dark hair. For all these differences, both men had the same weakness—the strong desire to lead the community in communal prayer.

Despite my great grandfather's age, with the help of the community, Yakov always made it to the lectern first. My grandfather Avrom would head for the door, but from that position would sing the responses with the most ornate flourishes and lengthily held notes. This was so that the community would compare his young and sweet voice with his father-in-law's hoarse one and regret that he wasn't leading them. Yet, despite Yakov's hoarse voice, his hoarseness had so many emotional tones and meanings that the community, including Avrom, wept when he prayed to God. Walking home with his two sons (my father and his brother,

Itsik) however, my grandfather Avrom still grumbled angrily that his father-in-law's praying was worthless and that there was no expert in davening on the entire street.

This poem was layered with meaning for me. Apart from the familial personality characteristics it reveals, it is the only anecdote I have about my father's teenage years that provides some details about my father's religious upbringing. In addition, here he is with his brother, Itsik, who isn't mentioned by name in the poem but appears as one of my grandfather's two sons, beside their father on the walk home from *shul* (synagogue). I learned that there was typically a prayer house on almost every street, and often more depending on which religious tradition the community followed, where prayers were led by members of the community. I could see my father as a teenager in this domestic scene and anticipate his struggles with his father and with religious tradition.

After my mother's death, when I became more proactive in investigating both my mother's and father's histories, I asked my father questions that focused on how he survived the war and met my mother. I knew only the bare outlines of his life in the suburbs of Vilna as a young man helping his family in their inn. I never asked him about his early childhood, his relationship with his siblings, or his religious education. I never asked him details about when and why he gave up religious practice. These poems scattered through several books, although sparse in their details about family members, nevertheless filled in some of the blanks, and I was glad to have found them.

My father wrote very little about his older brother, Itsik. Apart from the above poem, he only appears in two other poems, one of them a beautiful poem entitled "*Alts iz yidish*" (Everything Is Yiddish).

The theme of this deeply spiritual poem is how everything in my father is wrapped in Yiddish: his grandfather's blessing over his grandmother's goblet of juice, the bags containing his father's prayer shawls embroidered by his mother, and the remarkable, glowing language that has not been extinguished in him. Rhymes in Yiddish come to him like holiday guests. And when his inner light becomes blue with melancholy and exhaustion, that is when his Yiddish poem begins to weave within him. He likens this experience to the curtain that covers the ark holding the Torah scrolls and the clouds that bedeck the heavens parting to reveal the sun. He explains more in this verse:

> My father's melody and my sister's Bundist song,
> they all lie guarded in me,
> my mother's Sabbath candles
> and my brother's hora dance
> those are the human lights
> that shine and gleam within me.

My *tante* (aunt) Etke, the sister singing the Bundist song, was the only one of my father's six siblings who survived the war. She continued to live in Montreal after we moved to Toronto but was still in my life for many years, dying a few years before my father. I asked her on several occasions to speak about her experiences during the war. Each time, she would begin to relate some details, but then begin to weep and tell me that she couldn't continue. It wasn't from her or from my father that I found out that a child had been taken from her in the Vilna ghetto. I was told this much later, from a friend of the family who had survived the Vilna ghetto liquidation.

My father spoke very little about his only brother, Itsik. He told me in our recorded interview that Itsik died under Nazi occupation working in the peat bogs. Itsik was five years older than my father, the second oldest in a family of seven children. That is the sum of information I knew about Itsik prior to reading this poem.

After reading the poem, I learned that the Eastern European and klezmer horas were different from the hora that emerged in Palestine and Israel and later spread to wedding celebrations in North America. Itsik's hora dance was danced to a Yiddish melody and made an impression on my father. I'm glad to know that my uncle Itsik liked to dance.

Peretz Miransky and Shmerke Kaczerginski, pre-war Vilna.

Yung-Vilne; Miransky is third from left, back row.

Lola and Peretz, post-war Berlin.

Peretz Miransky, New York, 1960.

Miransky family, New York, 1960.

Saba and Peretz, Toronto, late 1970s.

Chapter 6: A Friendship—
Chaim Grade

Early in this project, I came upon four consecutive poems about Chaim Grade in my father's last published book, *A zemer fun demer* (A Melody from the Evening). Three are simply titled "Chaim Grade" and the fourth is called "*Shats dem dikhter*" (Value the Writer). I was immediately drawn in by the poem's descriptions of Grade's and his mother's lives in Vilna and also by a mystery surrounding his death that my father alluded to but did not spell out clearly.

Grade, like my father, was a member of *Yung-Vilne*, and like my father survived the Holocaust in the Soviet Union. He gained renown as a poet in Vilna before the war and went on to become a prolific and well-known poet, playwright, and novelist.

According to the YIVO (Institute for Jewish Research) *Encyclopedia of Yiddish Literature*, Grade ranks among the most important Yiddish writers of the post-Holocaust period, remembered for the richness of his prose and his depictions of both rabbinic high culture and life on the Jewish streets of Vilna. Many in the Jewish literary world consider his work superior to that of I. B. Singer, who crossed the language divide and won the Nobel Prize for literature.

Following the war, Grade lived in New York with his second wife, Inna Hecker Grade, and he visited my father in Toronto. My father talked about him as his closest friend. His love, admiration, and respect were obvious in how he spoke and wrote about him. I remember being introduced to Grade by my father. I remember the cloud that seemed to hover over him. He seemed deeply depressed.

In these four poems, my father describes Grade's extreme poverty growing up as a child and the physical misery of his surroundings. He describes how Grade's mother, Vella, eked out a living selling apples by the gate of the blacksmith's forge where they lived. He speaks of the burden of guilt Grade carried for surviving when his wife and mother were murdered. Grade was a deeply devout man, and according to my father's poems, he held the belief that his life had to be shackled to pain and horror for abandoning his wife and mother in his flight to escape the Nazi invasion of Vilna.[1]

In his poems, my father lauds Grade's prolific creative gift and honors him for immortalizing Vilna's markets, synagogues, and inhabitants, for memorializing the city in its poorest and most exalted places, and for elevating Yiddish in his writing.

And then comes the mystery: Why has Grade's memory not been preserved at least with a plaque? Why has such a wonderful writer not been given his due? The questions intensify in the second poem: Why is the community silent about his death and why is his death not commemorated? Where are the community leaders and why have they been silent for so long in denying Grade his due honor? In the third poem, the question becomes more personal. Why has his friend been denied the honor that he deserves?

He, my father, would, out of love and justice, have wanted to accompany Grade's coffin to give him a last kiss, to express his pain and regret. In the fourth and final poem, my father is at his most explicit. One can have justifications and reasons for anger, but how is it possible to take revenge on a dead writer? The man and the writer are two beings in one body. Death obliterates one, but the writer remains for eternity. So why are they both stuffed

---

1. Grade, *My Mother's Sabbath Days*, xi. Chaim Grade, like my father, did not believe that the Nazis would harm women and children. This was based on their experience when the German army occupied Vilna during Word War I.

in one grave? The last verse closes, "I do not demand in your pain that you love the man. But value the writer and the glowing light that remains with us." These forceful lines seem to be directed to someone specific.

I knew three things after reading these poems: that I wanted to know the story behind these poems, that I wanted to travel to New York to find and stand at Chaim Grade's grave, and that I wanted to read the letters Grade wrote to my father. The letters are held in the YIVO archives. I knew this because I brought the letters there myself in the years after my father died. It never occurred to me at that time to try to read what Grade had written my father, but I was eager to investigate the letters after I read my father's poems about Grade.

I traveled to New York in November 2021 and again in March 2023 for this specific purpose. By this time, I had learned about Chaim Grade's second marriage, to Inna Hecker. On my second trip, in March 2023, I came upon an article in the *New York Times* authored by Joseph Berger. Berger wrote what I had heard others say: that scholars believe that Grade never attained the crossover success achieved by I. B. Singer because of the obstacles to publishing English translations that Inna Hecker Grade imposed. For starters, she refused to allow scholars access to his papers after his death. Moreover, she kept the details of Grade's funeral secret, which was the mystery alluded to in my father's poems and explained his grievances about Grade being insufficiently honored.

I don't know if my father ever traveled to New Jersey to stand beside Grade's grave in the years after Grade died in 1982 and before his own death in 1993. But his grief at not being able to do so at the time of Grade's death comes through in his poetry, as these lines from the third "Chaim Grade" poem reveal:

> I would have accompanied you to the cemetery
> with love, in my correct place
> and have given you a last kiss,
> with pain, with tears and with regret.

My father's grief about this loss and about this missed opportunity for closure was surely intensified by the impossibility of attending funerals of friends and family who were murdered in the Holocaust, in Soviet prisons, and the Gulag, and by all the missing gravesites of family members and companions.

On a sunny November day, Dovid and I traveled by Uber to New Jersey, to the Riverside Cemetery where Grade is buried. Making our way to the grave site, we saw deer grazing between the stones. Because of the stories I had heard, I had expected to find a crumbling, neglected plot. But at Grade's grave site we found a simple memorial stone at the head of a sectioned marble slab running along the ground on which a long poem is engraved. The poem is a love ode to Vilna, which asks who will be able to resurrect its magic now that its last chronicler, Grade himself, has died. It speaks to Vilna directly, closing with these four lines:

> You hear me from the distant stars,
> with your sweet smile.
> Oh well of mine, of tears that have not yet been spent!
> My home without a tombstone, my eternal sanctuary!

I understood even more now the bond between Grade and my father, who shared the same sorrow. The depth of this particular bond was illuminated further in Grade's letters to my father, which were not as I imagined. I assumed that Grade's letters would be full of personal and intimate details about his life. I also imagined that he and my father would be in an ongoing discussion about Yiddish literature, commenting on what they were reading and engaging in conversations about the state and fate of Yiddish literature in the United States and Canada.

The letters from Grade to my father span the years from 1946 to 1980. They describe a relationship of mutual support, punctuated by grievances. Many letters dealt with the difficulty of raising the money necessary to publish and promote their works. Money loomed as an issue for them both. Grade supported himself solely through writing and lecturing. He wrote vividly about how meager the honorariums were, and how difficult it was for him to ask for higher fees. Raising the money to publish a book required a committee. Both my father and Grade were active in offering one another advice about whom to contact in their respective cities to organize a committee, arrange a lecture, make a book order, or find a place to stay overnight during a book tour.

But this process caused friction and illuminated some of their vulnerabilities and values. For example, my father felt slighted when Grade came to speak in Toronto and didn't stay with our family but rather with Kalman Berger.[2] Grade offered reasons having to do with his medical condition and reminded my father that it was he who had initially put him in touch with Berger as a potentially useful contact. In another letter, Grade responded to an accusation that he was kowtowing to the rich people in Toronto because he had again spent a night at Berger's home. He reiterated that my father was responsible for the contact with Berger, that he had in fact insisted that he was the best support for Grade.

Grade responded to another issue raised by my father following a lecture Grade had given at a Vilna Ghetto commemoration in Tel Aviv in 1963. My father was upset that Grade did not tell him about all the people from Vilna who asked about him, and that he didn't bring my father's address along, so that when people asked about my father, Grade was unable to provide it to them.

I was able to see in these disputes some of the same sensitivities that revealed themselves in my father's fables. Underneath my father's accusations were his vulnerabilities about being valued as he should be, for his "deep roots," his hard work and skill, and his persistence in maintaining and developing traditional forms, rather than by the standards set by a culture that overvalued financial success. He seemed to interpret innocuous behavior through this lens. His accusations also spoke to his need to be connected to others who shared his memories of Vilna.

---

2. Kalman Berger is mentioned several times in these letters as a potential source of financial and organizational support for publishing books in Yiddish. He was one of the original founders of the Bialik Hebrew Day School in Toronto.

In three of the letters from Grade to my father, Grade reiterated their bond by reminding him of the same shared memory. In the first of these, dated 1959, responding to a grievance of my father, he wrote: "We are old friends from Vilna. I remember how you stood by my mother's basket and recited your poem by memory, you standing next to my mother." He added: "We never fought, argued. Now for sure we won't." He offered this memory in three separate letters, responding to three separate situations—when he was frustrated by my father's complaints, to emphasize how close they were, and when he was touched by my father's care.

In a 1966 letter, written from the Burke Rehabilitation Center, where he was recovering from a heart attack, Grade wrote that he was deeply moved by my father's letter to him. Once again, he mentioned the bonding experience of reading poetry to one another when standing at his mother's gate.

Before my father's second book came out in 1974, letters from Grade referred to my father's poetry. He said he was organizing a committee to help my father publish this book. He sometimes critiqued his poetry, claiming, for example, that a strong opening line was squandered with a forced rhyme. He also quoted lines that he found to be strong.

Prior to the publication of the book devoted solely to fables, published in 1979, Grade referred to my father's "poetic proverbs," which he said were getting better and better.[3]

After my mother died in 1970, Grade sent a letter to my father attempting to console him. He offered advice to *"shtreng zikh on un shrayb lider"* (make every effort and write poetry). He said that my mother would have expected this of him. He suggested that my father should write about my mother and publish a book.

At the time of this letter, almost twenty years had passed since the publication of my father's first book in 1951. At the 1974 Montreal book launch of my father's second book, he said that he had written this book, among other reasons, so that his

3. Examples of this new poetic fable form developed by my father are described in chapter 3.

frozen tears could begin to flow. It seems thankfully, that he took Grade's advice.

Although I didn't find the personal conversations about their lives that I had been anticipating, Grade's letters to my father alluded to the intimate details of their lives. They were close enough to both squabble and make up.

Both men longed for Vilna. Both men mourned loved ones. Both were religious exiles, who lived with and processed their religious upbringing in different ways. They were intimate friends and spiritual companions bound to one another in their love and longing for their lost world.

Chapter 7: Within Himself

My father had a strong moralistic streak, which revealed itself frequently in judgments of others. Many of those judgments were reflected in the fables he wrote. Yet there was an aspect of this personality trait that meant a great deal to me personally. This was my father's willingness to hold himself accountable, and to apologize for behavior that didn't meet his own standards. In other words, the positive side of his moralistic streak was his willingness to put his own behavior under the microscope and take responsibility for it.

In reading his poetry, I discovered that the greatest victim of my father's judgment was himself. A short poem reveals his familiarity with this internal critic, and its relentless presence. "*Mayn shotn*" (My Shadow) was translated into English by my father and edited by Marvin Schiff. It reads as follows:

> I am always at war with my shadow
> whose face remains hidden from me,
> though he treads my path as I tread it
> and he ages like my effigy.
>
> Every night I awake to his whisper
> and by day he is there stubbornly.
> He arouses in me deep discomfort
> yet I carry him always with me.

It infuriates me, this bold mocking
of my spirit, my humanity.
I deflect his dark wisdom with logic,
'though I know that my shadow is me.

One of the first poems I read in my father's last book, *A zemer fun demer* (A Melody from the Evening), surprised me with information I had never suspected. It is called "*Kh'hob zikh aleyn*" (I Have Only Myself). My father is transparent in the poem about his regret for having lost friendships, especially the friendships of other writers. He speaks about his pride as an "illness," one he has suffered from for years. He longs both for the friendship of other Yiddish writers and good friends in general. Yet he cannot bring himself to make the first move, to write his feelings, perhaps his apologies, in a letter. They remain in his heart, and here in this poem. I wondered if he hoped that the poem would be read and be taken as an apology.

In the YIVO archives, I found among my father's papers an unsent letter to Avrom Sutzkever,[1] a well-known Yiddish poet and member of *Yung-Vilne*, the literary group to which my father belonged in Vilna. The letter expressed some hurt and anger about Sutzkever's response to a request my father had made. It shed some light on my father's sensitivities and made me wonder about the hurts he could not share and why. I was reminded of moments when I knew he was hurt and I saw his face go still. If asked what was wrong, he might shake his head and refuse to answer. My father struggled expressing grief and hurt in personal encounters, to me and, apparently, to others.

Other poems reveal that he saw his father as suffering from the same "illness" of stubborn pride and believed that he had inherited this personality trait from him. In "*Tate mayner*" (My Father), discussed in chapter 2, my father points out there wasn't peace between them, that they were both stubborn and that this stubbornness divided and separated them. In a poem entitled "*Ikh hob*

1. For more information about Sutzkever and the unsent letter, see chapters 8 and 10.

a shtoltz" (I Have Pride), my father confesses that he has a "manly pride" that doesn't let him bend. He acknowledges in the poem that he knows that this was inherited from his father.

These poems, in which he reflects on his personality characteristics and how they have influenced his life and relationships, are filled with regret. Perhaps one of my father's most profound regrets was about his failure to teach his children to speak Yiddish and to carry on his legacy. There were probably many reasons for this, including that he was often away from home when we were growing up. And as he revealed in his own poetry, he was always reluctant interpersonally to put his feelings and needs into words, particularly those that were most important to him.

A poem entitled "*Al khet shekhotosi byidish*" (For the Sin that I Have Sinned against Yiddish) reveals how intense his feelings of regret for this omission were and how they persecuted him. The phrase "for the sin that I have sinned" is a confession of sins repeated ten times in the course of the Yom Kippur services. My father uses this phrase to confront and castigate himself and those like him for the sin that was sinned against Yiddish. Unlike pious Jews who preserved their traditions, my father's generation didn't guide their children to retain the Yiddish language. We, his children, weren't taught to believe, to esteem our cultural wealth and experience how it could ennoble and elevate us, and that is why, he claims, that today we worship false gods. He describes the pain of this recognition vividly, as birds of prey that came in the night to peck him with their sharp talons and beaks. This guilt was intense and caused him enormous pain.

The guilt was intense in me as well. I remember a public event commemorating the Holocaust during which my father read his poetry. At the end of it, standing near the exit, we were approached by a member of the audience, who greeted my father. He turned to me and spoke about how my father was able to put into words his (the listener's) feelings and the feelings of others who had survived the Holocaust. He asked me in an accusatory tone why it was that I didn't speak Yiddish. I felt, as I always did when I heard this question, both guilt and shame. But by this point in my life, I was able to muster a self-defensive response. I responded that perpetuating a language is a parental responsibility and not something a child decides. My father, standing nearby, overheard the conversation and nodded, adding, "*Gerekht*" (That's right).

My father openly revealed other things about himself in his poetry, including his aspirations for himself as a human being. One of my favorite poems, entitled "*Lern mikh*" (Teach Me), is familiar as I had included it in *Peretz Miransky: Selected Poems and Fables*, published in 2000.

But I read it differently now while undertaking this project, as an authentic inner prayer written by a poet whose spiritual striving to do good and be good was at his absolute center. The English translation by Marvin Schiff retains its poetry and soulfulness:

> Teach me, God, to remember
> all my yesterdays, which lie in dust and ember,
> all the turnings of my stormy past.
>
> Teach me to remember all my wrongings,
> the wild eruptions of my longings,
> that I might come to myself at last.
>
> I went out seeking dreams and revels,
> in the deepest valleys, at the highest levels.
> I sent my steps to every distant ground.
>
> 'Til with the sum of all my years' existence,
> I discovered not in some radiant distance,
> but in the human heart's where God is found.
>
> So I beg you, shape my life, my living.
> Teach me how to be a giver, giving
> All I have, the holdings of my lot.

Teach me how to keep my giving steady.
Let me be willing, always ready,
That I may be worthy, that you may live within me, God.

There are poems that describe what my father encountered within himself when he entered his body in order to write. In a very compressed poem entitled "*Ikh bin a siluet*" (I Am a Silhouette), my father claims that as a poet, he writes "in blood" with a prayer upon his lips yet hears a lamenting hyena in his remotest depths. He reveals that whenever he is alone with himself and his shadow, he senses a bitterness in his bones, bones that are covered in grey ash. Then he asks why his disposition is so full of temptation and struggle. Why does he have to struggle to the death with his poems and fables? As soon as an idea is sprouted in him, as if a wild seed, he feels compelled to sweat and wrestle with his dream, like Jacob on the ladder. It doesn't help to plead; his voice is not heard. His sunset has split into two and bleeds, just as his raw words do.

My father writes in this poem about his inner struggle with the desire and compulsion to write, to honor and continue his legacy, to realize his dream, and the bloody destruction that was with him in every theme he wrote. My father never wanted to be the poet who chronicled and described the catastrophe of the Holocaust, but he obeyed the calling of his muse and his conscience in his writing, wherever it took him or whatever it cost him.

A short poem entitled "*Ikh vil nit zayn*" (I Don't Want to Be) lays out who my father wanted to be in his writing, and in his life:

Oh God, I don't want to be a parrot
repeating all the sages' chatter.
I want to howl like a wolf in the snowy night
and wake the world up with my cry.

The woods are full of silence and of fear.
The winter has bedecked its light green skin
and in his city, lurking bloody red,
lives the hunter and the fear of death.

I don't want to be the hunter or the gun
nor do I want to be the deer. I want to be a quiet bush
that dreams in the snowy silver spray
of spring, which surely comes one day.

In this poem, my father expresses his desire for his writing to be original, rather than something regurgitated and repeated. He wants his writing to howl like a wolf, wild and compelling enough to wake the world up to itself. He places the hunter and his violence in the city, not the beautiful countryside of his memories. If there is a choice to be made between perpetrator or victim, he chooses to be neither. He chooses beauty and the dream of a better world.

Another poem, entitled "*Kholem oys*" (Dream Up), reveals something of my father's strategy for survival given the burden of loss he carried. In the first verse, my father exhorts himself to "dream up a white tree, which is always in bloom," with a twittering bird perched upon it. He follows this verse by describing a dark sky with all its stars sleeping. Only one star, a tear actually, is keeping its eye open. And as it turns out, the owner of this tear is God, God who has leased his land to Satan, a devil who is bloodthirsty and takes pleasure in horror.

When God arises at midnight for study and prayer in remembrance of the destruction of Jerusalem, he perceives his great error. Consequently, God extinguishes all the stars, leaving only one to weep for God's mistake. The poem concludes that it is difficult for a soulful person to live without dreams and a night without stars is dreadful. The poem ends as it begins: "So dream up a white tree which is always in bloom."

The poem is rich with historical and mystical meaning. The word used for "lease" (*arende*) is a Yiddish word for the practice in Eastern Europe when Jews were serfs under a feudal system. And God, like pious Jews steeped in kabbalistic practice, arises at midnight for prayer and study as they did. My father gives us a clue about how to survive terrible trauma. He used poetry and his imagination to create a beautiful myth, so he could go on.

I also learned about my father from the themes that were not in his poetry. I realized at one point that I had read almost all the way through his life work and had yet to encounter a poem that cried for revenge, for bloodshed.

Close to the end of his life, during one of his last hospital stays, my father told me that when he returned to Vilna after the war, he found the home of the farmer who had betrayed the hiding place of his family to the Nazis. He went to the farmer's house for three nights in a row with a gun, hovering under his window, debating with himself about whether or not to kill him. He left, finally, deciding not to. He asked me if he had done the right thing. I said "yes," although I remember that the rest of my answer was clumsy.

I wish I had said then, as I would say to him wholeheartedly now, that such an act would have betrayed who he was in his core. My father was peace-loving by nature, wanting, as he declared in a number of poems, to stretch out his hand and live in harmony with his countrymen and neighbors. This act of murder, had he accomplished and gotten away with it, would have haunted him. Yet this post-war encounter in Vilna and this question about avenging the murder of his family remained with him as an un-answered question until the very end of his life.

Chapter 8: Yiddish

My father grew up in Vilna, known as "Jerusalem of Lithuania" for its significant Jewish population and cultural atmosphere.[1] Vilna is historically understood to be the capital of Lithuania, but it was annexed by Poland between the two world wars. Though under Polish rule, Vilna remained the undisputed capital of Lithuanian Jewry and was celebrated as the cultural center of Eastern European Judaism. The city's cultural importance far exceeded its size. A lively and rich Yiddish cultural scene developed and flourished there.

Several Yiddish newspapers and literary magazines were published in Vilna. The Yiddish literary group *Yung-Vilne* was inaugurated there in 1929 and Yiddish music and theatre groups, libraries and schools, flourished there. After World War I, Yiddish writers gave lectures to the public and mentored students, such as my father, who were seeking their own poetic voices.

Vilna was the birthplace of several important cultural and religious institutions. The YIVO Institute[2] was founded in Vilna in 1925 to further the study of the Yiddish language as well as Jewish culture and society. The Bund[3] was founded in Vilna in 1897, and Rabbinic culture flourished there alongside Yiddish secular culture. The prevalence of Yiddish and Yiddish cultural

1. Zalkin, "Vilnius."

2. Kuznitz, "YIVO."

3. Blatman, "Bund."

production in Vilna is essential to understanding my father's life before and after the Holocaust.

Many of the poems my father wrote about the creative process are expressions of wonderment and joyous affirmation of the mysterious power that filled him with Yiddish words yet required his effort and skill to reach their ultimate expression. But some of these poems about the creative process are also soaked in grief for what had been lost.

The odes to Yiddish are among the most beautiful and sad poems I read, filled with love, affirmation, and spiritual depth. Yiddish was a lover that my father knew intimately—he idolized her; he knew her other admirers; he knew her history and the miracle of her creation as a literary language. He celebrated her attributes. He was grief-stricken at her demise.

My father wrote many poems about other Yiddish writers. Some of these writers were familiar to me, while others were not. Some perished in the Holocaust or were killed in Stalin's prisons and gulags. Others escaped Europe and lived in Montreal or New York, contemporaneously with my father.

The first of the odes to Yiddish I read is "*Dos yidish lid*" (The Yiddish Poem), in my father's 1974 book, *Shures shire* (Lines of Song), within a section called "*Lidershaf*" (Poem Creation). "*Dos yidish lid*" describes Yiddish as a lowly servant that the writers Mani Leib, Itsik Manger, Avrom Reisen, Peretz Markish, and H. Leivik adorned and beautified with the magic of their craft. Under their spell, Yiddish became a princess, until she was banished behind seven black mountains and behind seven seas, as described in the following passage:

> And there, in a flaxen shirt, abandoned and forgotten,
> the Yiddish princess wanders like a beggar.
> She goes around in her red crown of wilted roses
> and waits for a good prince from far away to come and revive her.

Many of the poems, as in this one below, simply titled "*Yid-dish*," are full of grief for a lost love and the futility of trying to resurrect her:

I have kissed you with scorched lips
from shamed ghettos and dead marshes
and brought you with me, like a crying child
Yiddish, mother tongue, seeking an heir.

This poem ends in a place of deep discouragement, with a sense of futility about what my father continued—needed—to do in order to keep himself whole and to stay connected to who he was. The closing lines read:

What words of comfort will I tell myself today
as my reality and dream is not worth a penny!
How much longer can I carry you on my lips?
Yiddish, my mother, language of suffering and song.

In the next poem, also titled "*Yiddish*," there is a shift to a sliver of hope, a pattern I noticed again and again. My father came close to drowning in his sorrow, and yet his writing saved him because it connected him to what was most valuable in his life: his purpose as a link in the golden chain, his culture, his language, and, equally important, his own creative process, which filled him with wonderment and allowed him to be most deeply himself. He writes:

Even today, you beautify our Diaspora,
and he who believes in you and lives,
opens up his hands and coattails
like blue wings and glides

over houses, over stables,
free and far from restriction and predicament,
like in Chagall's paintings,
like in the Baal Shem's stories.

In *Shures shire*, I found a series of poems dedicated to other Yiddish writers, in sequence: Leivik, Itsik Manger, Yankev Glatshteyn, Der Treyster (Leyeles), Avrom Sutzkever, Rokhl

Korn, Melekh Ravitsh, and Israel Emiot, some of whom I had previously heard of, or heard my father speak of, while others were unknown to me. I paid particular attention to the poems about these writers that seemed the most deeply personal and heartfelt: Leivik and Rokhl Korn. I was still seeking to understand my father, to know who influenced him and why, and these writers offered a window into his lost world.

Leivik[4] (1888–1962) was one of the most renowned Yiddish poets, and he was also greatly admired for his convictions and his humanity. He became a member of the Bund in 1905 but was arrested in 1906 and jailed in Minsk. He was sentenced to four years of hard labor and then perpetual exile in Siberia. On the day of his trial, he refused to take part in his defense, saying to the court that everything he had done he had done with full consciousness, and he would do everything he was capable of to undermine the tsarist autocracy.

He was marched to Siberia in a convict procession, a journey that took four months. He arrived at Vitim in 1912, a village in the middle of a forest where winter lasted for nine months of the year and darkness lasted eighteen hours of the day. In 1913, he was assisted to escape by colleagues in the United States who sent him money, which he used to buy a horse and sled to make a long journey to a railway line.

He arrived in the United States at the age of twenty-four. Like my father, Leivik cherished the spiritual core of Judaism and sought to make it the focus of a renewed modern Judaism. His ideas about spiritual redemption in the modern world appeared in his poems and plays and were widely debated.

Leivik died in 1962, twelve years before this poem (entitled "*Leivik*") appeared in my father's second book. Likely, it was written around the time of his death. In the poem, my father first speaks to Leivik directly:

> …you purified yourself your entire life
> in the glow of snow and the secret of silence

4. Denman, "Leivick."

until a pure being, you travelled far away
on your way to God . . .

The cultivation and maintenance of silence is a tool of mystical experience. Leivik had a stroke in 1958 and lost his power of speech until his death four years later. Poet friends would visit and read to him during this time. Yet amongst his friends, there was some debate about whether he was unable to speak or was simply choosing not to.

Addressing Leivik's mourners from the perspective of his literary and spiritual contributions, the poem closes by saying:

only his remembrance candle remains,
his song, with us, in the deepest depths,
in his kinfolk, in body and soul
for all time.

The power of spiritual and cultural inheritance is laid out succinctly in these four lines. I wondered whether my father sought consolation and guidance from Leivik's writing at the times of his own most profound suffering.

Unlike the poems about other writers in this section, entitled *"Lidershaf"* (Poem Creation), my father dedicated his poem about Rokhl Korn to her (*"Tsu Rokhl Korn"*) and inscribed it, *"far ir bukh, Di genod fun vort"* (for her book, The Grace of Words).

Rokhl Korn[5] (1898–1982) was my father's contemporary, born ten years earlier than him, on a farming estate in Eastern Galicia (Western Ukraine). Although Polish was the language of her household, she began writing and publishing in Yiddish after the First World War. She was acclaimed both for her poems on nature and love and lauded for her successful portrayals of the peasantry, both Jewish and non-Jewish. She felt deeply rooted to the land on which her ancestors had lived for generations alongside Polish-speaking neighbors and farmers, until the displacement and persecution of the Holocaust.

5. Frank, "Korn, Rokhl."

Like my father, Korn escaped the Nazis by fleeing to the Soviet Union. Her entire family was killed except for her daughter, and, like my family, she moved to Montreal in 1949. After the war, her poems became odes to what was lost and vehicles to express her pain and longing. She was a visitor to my father's home in Toronto and I remember him speaking admiringly about her work. The poem about Rokhl Korn reads as follows:

> Sometimes you hear more in someone else's words
> and someone else's confession becomes your own secret.
> I have in your leaf fall heard myself,
> and thank you for your singing words of grace.
>
> In hours when the seconds become greyer
> and windows become foggy and blind,
> it's good to drink your sadness
> and glow like an autumn tree in the wind.
>
> I glow with your whispering words in my ear
> with your tears which burn and heal like iodine.
> I thank you for your "autumn tears."
> I thank you for all your words of grace.

In reading this very personal confession, I became aware that my father saw Korn as a kindred spirit, both in her devotion to the earth in which she was rooted and in her grief for what was lost forever.

Yiddish and creation were inseparable for my father and poems about Yiddish are often placed in the sections of his books describing the creative process. A poem in *Shures shire* (Lines of Song) entitled "*Trit*" (Steps) is found in a section labeled "*Shternksav*" (Star Writing). In it, the poet describes himself as a *mindster* (the little finger of a hand, or the smallest one), and a *blinster* (the blindest one). In this context, he seems to be expressing how small he feels as a human being and a spiritual seeker. He paces in the night, seeking everything that human beings have ever imagined.

"The wolf drags memories of bright clear days to its den," and my father's dream, the dream he once shared with others, which he called "our consolation," has been lost.

The wolf dragging bright clear days to its den is a powerful image. I imagined my father being lost for a moment in happy memories, which were then covered with the knowledge of the annihilation to come. Here is the dream again, the dream that preoccupied his days and animated his nights. In this poem, his dream could be a yearning for social justice and/or the dream of an inspirational secular Yiddish culture.

He taps with his stick in an empty field, searching for the dream of the lost world. Lies and falsehoods rule the streets but the dreamers, those who want to awaken others, lie naked and hollow, their lips sealed. He returns to himself, walking in the twilight, with a pail. He draws whatever he can from the well but he cannot draw the dream. His poem follows his footsteps; they are both tired.

My father devotes a section of his 1983 book, *Nit derzogt* (Incompletely Expressed), to "*Shafers*" (Creators). There are poems here devoted to Yiddish writers who influenced him, both past and present. One of the earliest is entitled "*Kulbak*" and is a long poem in which he writes about one of his two major influences, his teacher Moyshe Kulbak.

Kulbak (1896–1937) was a Yiddish poet, novelist, and dramatist. During his years in Vilna, he was one of the most popular figures in Yiddish cultural life, and he was active in Yiddish cultural institutions. He taught Yiddish literature in the local Yiddish high schools and lectured at the Yiddish Teachers' Seminary.

Although it was Eliezer Shteynbarg who inspired my father to write fables, Kulbak was his poetry teacher. And unlike Shteynbarg, who lived in faraway Czernowitz, Kulbak was a local presence in his life.

The poem begins with a description of Kulbak, a dark lock of hair falling forward on his forehead, his eyes growing rounder as he stares into the distance, reciting his poem to a group of his students, who are bewitched by his words. The way he looks at and speaks to his students is nurturing, inspiring them to believe in their own writing.

Each of his students comes to him with his own notebook of poems and he, their teacher, friend, and consoler, teaches each one how to find themselves. He leads his students outdoors and teaches them to discover how to create poetry from the whisper of the wind, the sprouting of plants and the rustling of trees in the mountains and the valleys. Verses full of appreciation, love, and longing follow as these words attest:

> Ah, Kulbak, my teacher and intimate idol,
> Who would have believed then, that I
> the prankster, the brawler and swimmer
> would so completely fall in love with poems and rhymes?
>
> Like brilliant stars, his words about lines and melody
> took hold of me.
> My fables and poems have him to thank
> because everything I draw, I draw with his pail.
>
> Everything that I think is the effect of his dedication,
> everything I seek is his tearful destiny
> and everything that I want and dream, I find
> in his sparkling Yiddish words.

The poem then turns to describe Kulbak's imprisonment and execution under Stalinist repression in 1937. It bewails the loss of Yiddish that Jews forget, mock, and ridicule, thereby desecrating the illuminated names of murdered Jewish fellow poets. He closes by writing:

> My blood cries with chagrin
> that my language just like my poem is disowned and shamed.
> I carry my language on my lips in order to defy my generation,
> that is blind to the beauty of Yiddish.

My father emphasizes his loss by describing and contrasting the blazing light of Kulbak's inspiration with the tragedy of his personal fate and the fate of Vilna's Yiddish culture and language. Of all the love poems my father has written, this one to his teacher is the one that describes the beloved with the most intimate details and burns with the strongest passion.

Also in this section is a long poem entitled "*Vogler*," about Elkhonen Vogler, who was a leading poet in *Yung-Vilne*. Vogler had a tragic early life, having lost both parents by the age of eight. Elsewhere, my father describes how Vogler retreated into nature and silence. But in this poem, he describes some of his personal interactions with him.

The poet writes that he was three years younger than Vogler and was still writing secretly while Vogler was already a well-known poet. He describes Vogler with paint on his fingers from making a living as a sign painter. He writes that Vogler read his early poems to my father, slowly and quietly. And then my father is reminded of the beginning of one of Vogler's poems and puts the other poet's words directly into his own poem:

> Oh, carry me, longing, to a land
> where a blind musician lives
> who plays melodies from my life on a flute

He remembers Vogler reading him this poem while the sun set over the tollgate in Shnipeshok, which defined the border of the city. And then, as in his ode to Kulbak, the poet closes the piece with the terrible and tragic irony of Vogler's fate. Vogler survived the loss of his parents as a child through nature and poetry, but his longing didn't lead him to a magical place where the sadness of his life could be expressed in music. It led him "to the ghetto gates, to streets smeared with blood" and finally to an attic in a foreign land, where the surrounding language was foreign, where the crowd in the city was unfamiliar, and where his light quietly burned out.

My father must have met Vogler in Paris, where Vogler remained after the war. My father, also a stranger in an unfamiliar city and foreign land, deeply understood Vogler's alienation and sorrow.

A very long poem, a ballad, longer by many pages than any other in my father's lexicon, closes this section. It is entitled "*Dos gesl fun zibn poetn*" (The Street of Seven Poets). It is an ode to the street on which my father lived, where, as he tells it, six other poets also lived, some of them well known and members of literary groups, and others not.

In the poem, my father takes the reader on a walk through his neighborhood, describing each house as he comes to it. He could still intimately picture the road, houses, and yards, and his descriptions show the reader both the physical and emotional environments in which these poets lived.

This is a very dense poem, in which a lot of information is presented. The tone is intimate and filled with details about the poets' homes and families. Sadly and inevitably, each of the verses describing the poets' homes ends with a different description of loss and destruction.

Avrom Sutzkever lives in the first house. My father tells us that he played chess with Sutzkever's brother and that his devout mother brought them refreshments with love on her face. He can still see Sutzkver sitting by the window, dreaming up "singing words . . . fresh from the garden bed." Rays of light come through the window forming a golden chain around Sutzkever's neck. But now, the poet writes, a chestnut tree "like a deformed menorah without candles" looks through the broken window frames.

Sutzkever was perhaps the most famous member of *Yung-Vilne*, a poet and partisan who, post-war, founded the literary quarterly *Di goldene keyt* (The Golden Chain) in Israel.

The next house he comes to is Leyzer Volf's, who was also a member of *Yung-Vilne*. He tells us how the "pen constantly wrangles with the needle" there, that "even his gloves are stitched with a rhyme." Although his drawers are filled with poems, his house is poor and empty, and his bitter anger causes him to turn to the "false redeemer," the promise of universal justice in the Soviet Union.

The third house he comes to is the home of the local rabbi, whose name is Basin. The rabbi has one child, who is not named but vividly physically described. The young man grows like a "thin, pale plant in a sandy garden bed" and always has such sorrow on his pale face. He is lonely and quiet and hides in the shadows. The street is curious about him and rumours spin. The rabbi reproaches his son, who interrupts his studies to pace around the room, keeping time on his fingers to the rhythms of his own poems. But moralizing, yelling, and punishing him doesn't correct his behavior. He continues to write poems despite his father's injunction. And he begins to meet with the other young scribblers who have dreams like his. At sunset, he goes to the banks of the Vilia river, from where his body is retrieved by a fisherman along with two notebooks of poems. These tragic verses may be all that remain of this young poet.

The fourth house is the home of *Auguzel der kleyner* (Auguzel, the small one). My father tells us that his viola is almost as big as him. His mother is a fisher and carries baskets of fish for sale on her arm. She is embarrassed to come into the room where the young poets are gathered and chatting around the table in the evening.

The fifth house is where my father lived, by the city gate at the foot of the Sheshkiner Hills. He describes the birch tree in his yard, bent over like a bow, the birch tree that appears in so many of his poems. His garden is sown with peas and carrots. His house is filled with the music of five sisters who sing constantly.

The sixth house, just across the road, holds a relative, the "beautiful and beloved . . . blond and young" poet Hirsh Glik. His father is a dealer in rags, a simple man with a dream in his gaze.

My father describes the poverty in Glik's house as "clean and concealed." But in this house, as in his own, love blooms. The poem describes how Glik goes to work at the age of thirteen to "drive the hardship from his home" and brings home a fresh loaf of bread at night "like a gift." When the Nazis invade Vilna, my father and Glik start off together, running fearfully in a desperate attempt to escape. But by the Sheshkiner Bridge, Glik comes to a standstill and runs back to his family, unable to abandon them, despite his fear. Ultimately, Glik dies as a partisan in the woods "with a rifle in his hands."

Only three houses past Glik's on the same street lives the poet Moyshe Gurin, the seventh and last poet in this poem, a cousin of Glik's and his classmate. The two of them link their homes and their pens in the dream of *Yungvald*.[6] Gurin survives the war, "he doesn't know how, himself," and writes "lamenting poems in Holon."

The last few verses are a pain-and-love-filled description of the demise of my father's little street "full of belief, dreams and markets." He describes how his road "rolled like a cask of fine wine from the Sheshkiner hills, until it rolled into the sunset, burning like a barrel of alcohol; and extinguished itself in the Vilye river, like a big, flaming sun." He writes:

> My days, blown away with poison and flame
> full of dreams, youth and debates.
> On a small cultivated street
> our young song sprouted.
>
> Seven young vibrant poets,
> full of hope, full of the pain of creation.
> Who was it that sowed seeds in three of them in late autumn
> as they were perishing, leaving them to blossom in the snow ...?

Of these seven Yiddish poets on my father's street, three survived the war: my father, Avrom Sutskever, and Moshe Gurin, who like Sutskever made his home in Israel after the war. These were the three surviving poets of Shnipeshok, who remembered and chronicled this neighborhood, this hub of creativity from within the depths of poverty that was nested within the richness of Vilna's Yiddish culture. Tragically, as my father wrote, they were destined

---

6. Cammy, "Volf, Leyzer." *Yungvald* (Young Forest) was a literary fellowship of teenage writers mentored by Leyzer Volf. Moshe Gurin and Hirsh Glik were members of *Yungvald*. Gurin survived the war and settled in Israel.

to blossom "in the snow" rather than in their original environment, which had nurtured their creative and spiritual growth.

In "*Mayn tatns nign*" (My Father's Melody), my father describes his father's morning prayer, sung to a melody that he still remembers. My father inserts Yiddish words into this melody and the Yiddish words resound as beautifully and tearfully as the prayers once did in Hebrew on his father's lips. He closes with a fearful question: "Will my children hear this melody when I am gone?" He sings his father's melody as he approaches his own death and knows the melody will rock him silently as he passes and will remain upon his grave.

The imagery of my grandfather, whom I never knew, beginning his day saying his prayers to a melody was deeply moving to me. It helped me understand something my father once said about a poem set to music being the highest form a poem can achieve. Even more moving to me was the idea of my father setting Yiddish words to my grandfather's prayerful melody—this joining of their spirits, this attempt to bridge their separate worlds with a song that contained both of their spiritual strivings.

I recently read an essay by Isaac Bashevis Singer,[7] who immigrated to the United States in 1935. In this essay, Singer focused on his earliest impressions of America. He wrote about having "the uncanny feeling that all my values, all my notions and emotions, were shattered. I was torn away from the roots without which literature cannot exist."

The essay was written much later in Singer's life, from the wisdom of perspective. In it he suggested that world literature had overlooked the human experience connected with immigration. He felt that up until then, there had been no author who evoked the singular, deep crisis of those forced to leave their country, their home, their mother tongue and begin life anew in a strange land. All immigrants, he believed, face a sudden loss of values, a confusion and irritation that takes years to heal and sometimes even generations. He believed that this crisis was especially profound when

7. Singer, "Immigation."

the immigrant was a writer who had lost the language in which his means of expression, culture, and history were embedded.

I felt the truth of these words both in my father's life and in my own. My father was an immigrant such as Singer described, a writer forced to live in a country that neither shared his traditions nor spoke his language. Moreover, there was no homeland to return to. So much of his poetry describes the pain of this separation from his home, his Yiddish-speaking community, and his culture. As for me, I have always had a nameless craving for community and belonging. English is my language of expression but it doesn't reach deep into my ancestral past or offer me the rich experiences of my ancestors' daily lives.

Chapter 9: Green Words

My father's first book, consisting of poems and fables written mostly prior to the war in Vilna, does not have a section of poems devoted entirely to nature. All of the subsequent ones do, except of course for his book devoted entirely to fables. But in his first book, in a chapter entitled "*Teg*" (Days), it is already possible to see the power nature had to move and inspire him. A simple poem called "*Shtiler*" (Quietly), dated Vilna 1938, when he was thirty years old, reveals his uncomplicated, receptive response to a starry night.

Quietly

trills

a nightingale

All the world is dreaming

There's just a diamond spray of light

a starry vastness gleaming

There's just a softly

laughing brook

murmuring to the meadows

and a silver shower of stars

is raining

raining

raining

Twelve years after this poem set in Vilna, in a poem written in Montreal, nature frames and surrounds a different emotional state. This poem, called "*Shneyfal*" (Snowfall), dated 1950, is dedicated to my mother. In it, my father is looking out the window at a snowfall, asking my mother if she can see and hear it. He doesn't want her to answer in words because her answer would disturb the white silence. He invites my mother to sit beside him at the window, where they will coo like doves do, with words like tears in their throats, forgetting themselves in all of this.

He describes the earth as being robed in flax and in wonderment of itself. The world is animated. It is a miracle worker that beholds its own creation, a tree trimmed in white. He ends the poem by describing the windowpane as a well, with the two of them being pails on iron ropes, tied together "somewhere in a myth." The poem concludes with a meditative line: "And white as a miracle are the depths."

The poem alludes to the miracle of their survival, their bond and their new life together, and it hints at sadness and things that need to be forgotten. But nature, covering everything in pure whiteness, can create miracles, lifting people out of themselves. It offers transcendence of personal suffering and is a source of consolation. The great "mysterious power" my father has written about elsewhere is in nature as well as in people.

In "*Zun un regn*" (Sun and Rain), also written in 1950, my father's relationship to nature is portrayed differently. In three stanzas, the poem describes the sun looking through a net of clouds. The clouds scud over blue lakes like wet rafts. But when the sun reaches a building, "a blind window glares upon a deaf roof." Inside the building, where the sun doesn't reach, the poet shows the reader:

> stretched out on a bed
>
> with his head on a cushion,
>
> a person is lying
>
> like a page ripped out of a book . . .

In urban Montreal, at this time, when nature meets my father's house, even the sun, the source of light and illumination, is "blind" and the roof is "deaf." Inside, there is only alienation. My father is not gazing at a starry sky, or even looking out the window at a snowfall. Here he is, separated from nature, from the abundance and ripe beauty that had been all around him in Shnipeshok. Nature is no longer only a source of wonderment, inspiration, and transcendent power. It has become a metaphor to express painful emotional and complicated spiritual themes.

As already noted, my father grew up in a suburb of Vilna called Shnipeshok. There was a toll gate there, a historic landmark that separated Vilna from the surrounding countryside. His family had an inn that boarded the horses of the local farmers when they came to sell their goods in the market.

While reading, I began to understand the familiarity my father had with the natural world, as a man who walked through the meadows and surrounding hills, fished in the Vilia river, saw the stars in an open sky, and grew up close to and among domesticated and wild animals.

Twenty-three years after his first book was published, my father's next book, *Shures shire* (Lines of Song), has a section devoted entirely to nature, as would all of his future books containing poetry. These poems reflect the power of nature in all its seasons, elements, and weather and describe nature as holding a mysterious power. My father uses the elements of nature as metaphors to convey spiritual wisdom and reflect upon life's different stages.

As when I read the fables, I was again taken by the vocabulary my father held for nature, including the specific names of trees, vegetation, birds, and animals, as well as descriptions of their habits.

My father's Yiddish-speaking generation in Eastern Europe was the first to have a real appreciation for nature and the vocabulary to describe it. Their appreciation of and desire to live life in nature was one of the ways they were different and in conflict with their more traditional parents. My father's generation lived in, enjoyed, and were inspired by nature, unlike their parents, whose lives were governed by the Torah's practices and proscriptions.

The earliest forms of Yiddish, which originated in Germanic-speaking territory, went on to spread with Jewish migrations across much of Central and Eastern Europe. But Yiddish developed differently in Eastern Europe from its origins in Germanic territory. Yiddish absorbed into its vocabulary words and structures from Slavic countries such as Poland, Ukraine, Belarus, and Russia.[1] One aspect of this change in vocabulary was the absorption into Yiddish of the words for flora and fauna. But it was not until late in the nineteenth century, during the time of Mendele Mokher Sforim (1836–1917), that these words entered into Yiddish literature. Mendele believed that nature is an expression of what is godly and that there should not be a division between nature and culture. In his works, Mendele infused nature with godly imagery to bridge the gap between the scholastic Rabbinic culture that governed Jewish life and the beauty and inspiration he found in nature.

In the nature poems of *Shures shire*, every season is a source of inspiration for my father, and gives rise to different feelings and ideas, from erotic love to dreams of the legacy he wanted to leave behind. And the Canadian landscape, by this point in my father's life, is also a source of inspiration, as in the following poem, "Der friling—der moler" (Spring—The Painter), translated into English by my father and edited by Marvin Schiff. It reads:

> Spring, the invisible painter,
> in sun gold, richly attired,
> is painting his grandest creation
> in fields for all to admire.
>
> He spreads his palette with oils
> in colours so vibrant they glow,
> and deftly he fashions a landscape,
> more enchanting than even Van Gogh.

1. Katz, "Yiddish."

A squeeze of a tube and the sky
has a rainbow, a great arching wonder.
His brushes give layers of colour
to mountains and valleys thereunder.

He dapples the meadows and treetops.
No artist is quite so surehanded.
His canvases show the world's beauty
more surely than ever Cezanne did.

In the past, I encountered the Master
in the old world, near Vilna, my town.
Even then I revered all his paintings.
I sensed their eternal renown.

Today in the glorious morning,
I encountered the Master once more,
In Canada, still painting pictures
near the mighty St. Lawrence's shore.

The river flows deep, cold and blue there,
Like ink from an upended well.
Beyond, in a line, lie foothills,
like camels, all kneeling and still.

Beside it rise two trees, twin poplars,
so close that their branches enfold
Both bow their heads to the painter,
His tunic still spangled with gold.

My father discovered that the Canadian landscape could also
be transcendent. What made it so, in the places he loved the most,
were its similarities to the landscape of his youth, including the river

and the foothills beyond. He also said that the woods in the Laurentians reminded him of the woods surrounding Vilna.

I remember a summer in a rented cottage as a young child near St Agathe, in the Laurentian mountains of Quebec. My father worked in Montreal during the week but would join us on weekends. He took us berry picking in the woods and fishing for sunfish and perch. We watched him gut the fish and, later, fry them.

We would wait by the shore as my father stood motionless in a rowboat, utterly absorbed with his fishing rod in the water. He would have to be called home for dinner, and he always seemed reluctant to leave his calm, solitary time.

After we moved to Toronto in 1955, we spent a few summers in Roches Point on Lake Simcoe. My father would go for long walks along the shore, coming home with pieces of driftwood, which he would later fashion into wooden sculptures. His love for nature was clear and obvious. He seemed at home and happiest there. Perhaps that is why those memories stand out so clearly.

Wychwood Park is located near our first Toronto home on Tyrrel Avenue, where we moved when I was seven years old. We skated in the park in the winter and played on a woody hill that sloped to the concrete-covered street below in the summer. Walking through the park with my father one day, he stopped by a tree we came to, picked a prickly green chestnut burr from a branch, and opened it with a penknife to show me the shiny brown nut inside. Taking the time to show me something in nature was a rare gesture on his part. To me, it seemed like one of his magic tricks.

After my father remarried in 1976, he and his wife, Saba, traveled to many countries and continents. I still recall the look on his face and the enthusiasm in his voice when he described the Rocky Mountains following his return from a trip there. In a very long poem titled "*Di rokis*" (The Rockies), my father describes the huge trees, majestic mountains, and clear lakes he has seen.

Back home in Toronto, in a poem titled "*Volknshpil*" (Cloudplay), my father describes what he sees on a walk with the family collie. He writes that the wind is a master sculptor, forming lions' heads and barking dogs out of clouds. He describes the harvested fields he passes through that smell of apple and mint. He closes the poem by writing, "It's good to be alone with beauty, with oneself and with God." The beauty of this day shines through in this poem but memories of the sights and smells of the Vilna countryside seem to have been interspersed into my father's present-day interpretation of Toronto.

My father created these "green poems" out of the elements of nature that were available, both in his surroundings and in his memories. The raw materials were the changing seasons, the weather patterns, the natural environment, and their interplay.

Some elements of nature, like the autumn and the winter frost, as well as the contrast of the natural world with the bare city landscape, are used as metaphors upon which to hang his ongoing concerns for his legacy. For example, in a poem called "*Harbst*" (Autumn), he describes how the wind has torn the leaves from an apple tree. The apple tree, whose leaves have yellowed early, has lived through the summer to reach its golden old age. Now, it waits silently for the winter. The poet continues, making a direct comparison:

> I too stand like him,
> with empty branches
> preoccupied and thoughtful
> with lips that are silent.

My father describes having "so many poems" crammed into drawers. He himself is burdened with unease and doubt about who will inherit his "desecrated being," his "harsh life," and the "dispossessed language of joy and song" that has filled his life. He closes, returning to the metaphor of the tree:

> The apples lie there,
> delicious and ripe,
> lost in the fog
> and spoiling in the shade.

Trees appear again and again in my father's poetry. Birch, fir, chestnut, spruce, maple, oak, alder, and linden are all there as are the leaves and blossoms of fruit trees. In his last book, *A Zemer fun demer* (A Melody from the Evening), the nature section is entitled *"Beymer redn"* (Trees Speak). Trees are admired for their stature, generativity, endurance, and simple beauty, as in a chestnut tree that awakens at dawn and opens its eyes to greet a spring day. But at this stage in my father's life, they also serve as metaphors for the process of aging, as their leaves yellow and their branches become covered with snow. So too do trees serve as metaphors for the process of creation in their fallow times and their greening and blooming times.

Nature appears everywhere in my father's poetry, not just in its own sections, where his poems are mostly full of wonder at the works of nature's creation. Nature also appears in other sections of his books as metaphors to express my father's greatest losses and grief about who he might have become without the trauma of the Holocaust, as well as his hope for what his children might achieve. A poem entitled *"Ingl mayns"* (My Son), was translated by him into English and edited by Marvin Schiff. The first two verses are as follows:

> What I longed to be and could not,
> I hope you will be, my son.
> All my yesterdays are shriveled,
> Your days are springtime, full of sun.
>
> I'm old and barren like a blasted fir;
> You're a pine tree, tall and lean.
> I'm full of tar and drying needles,
> You're the green bud of my dreams.

After describing his torment and guilt that his language is a stranger on my brother's lips, he expresses a fervent wish that his son will not betray all that he has brought from his homeland.

He begs him to "go farther than me, be the guardian of my burnt home of yesterday."

My brother Rami, addressed so explicitly in this poem, was only fifteen years old when our mother died. Unlike Libi and I, he continued to live with my father in the years after my mother's death and then with my father and Saba, until his own marriage. My father and Rami became close after my mother died. My father took on the role of single parent to an adolescent boy during the years they lived together, just the two of them, alone. Rami describes a positive, warm relationship with our father, due at least in part, I believe, to his easygoing nature, and his considerable gifts of empathy, helpfulness, and concern for others.

To my surprise, the landscape of nature appears as a powerful metaphor to describe a spiritual homecoming in a group of poems written on a visit to Israel. I had thought that my father had made only one trip to Israel, in 1988, to accept the Manger Prize for his poetry book *Nit derzogt* (Incompletely Expressed). These poems, however, were written more than a decade earlier as they were found in *Shires shire* (Lines of Song), published in 1974, in a section entitled "*Mir un zey*" (We and Them).

"We" is a word I have not encountered much in my father's writing. Where I have seen it before, it was in the context of his mission as a survivor, to continue to write in Yiddish and keep alive the dream of Judaism rooted in secular Yiddish culture with values derived from the ethical basis of the religion, from traditions, and from literature.

These poems written about Israel have a tone unlike anything else I have read. They are brimming with love, awe, and gratitude. They express a new energy and renewed optimism. Israel seems to have offered my father a place where he felt once more at home, where the spiritual landscape, if not the physical one, was familiar.

A poem entitled "Haifa" is one of the most beautiful I've read. "Haifa" is a long poem, in which the verses describing the beauty of Haifa are interspersed with his reflections of its meaning to him. Here is the first verse:

The ocean is a bed, and the Carmel—a cushion.
When night comes riding in, on a fresh, fluttering wind
from the infinite blue beyond,
God comes here to sleep.

He reflects that he has seen Haifa's beauty and his heart has stuttered, "Thank you for the privilege." Poems about Haifa's beauty have been told "in hundreds of generations and thousands of holy books." He confesses, "I have carried you in my heart and my memories."

And after further lyrical descriptions of roofs upon roofs and streets that wind upon a stone wall, where "houses crawl up hills like white elephants," he writes:

Palm trees sway—opened umbrellas.
The sea rocks itself and sings the Song of Songs.

A verse follows where he explains he came to Israel like a lyre without strings, as a survivor from Lithuania. He carries with him a painful song from there, from those "holy Jews burned in the fire." The final two verses describe a transformation, whereby new melodies have arisen in him, resounding with clarity and illuminated with light. He draws words from his depths, just as wooden pails draw crystal droplets from a well. It reads:

and I sing an original melody with ripe words
and the salt taste of tears.
You are as beautiful as a crown, set with stars,
ancient city of Haifa.

Here the loss of everything most cherished was bridged, in the living presence of these biblical sites, which were both part of his religious upbringing and the *Yiddishkayt* (Yiddish-ness) of Lithuanian Jewish culture, steeped as it was in biblical themes and characters. He was once more at home.

As always, when my father was most deeply stirred, he was the most deeply inspired. Nature had the power to move him to reflection and to mirror his wisdom, his wonder, his despair, and his hope. He let us know that this experience of being stirred by nature manifested within him as words that arose from his depths, his source. It was then that he felt most connected, to his ancestors, to his ancestry, and to himself. And this brought him joy.

Chapter 10: Song of Songs

As my father said, his two teachers when it came to writing fables and poetry were Eliezer Shteynbarg and Moyshe Kulbak. When he sat down to write, he could hear their voices and remember their words. They provided a template from which he was able to develop his own style.

But when it came to the poetry of romantic love, although Jewish Lithuania was the birthplace of modern Yiddish love poetry, my father did not borrow from any of the available models, including his teacher Kulbak or his cousin Hirsh Glik, instead relying on his own instincts.

In the *"Farfrorene trern"* (Frozen Tears) section of his book *Shires shire* (Lines of Song), published in 1974, my father included love poems full of grief and mourning for my mother, who had died four years prior to the book's release. He continued with the form after my mother's death. In his book *Nit derzogt* (Incompletely Expressed), published nine years later, he included poems that spanned the courtship and first years of his marriage to his third wife, Saba. Those poems are found in a section titled *"Shir ha shirim"* (The Biblical Song of Songs).

My parents came from very different worlds. My grandfather on my mother's side, Samuel, had been a successful textile merchant in St. Petersburg. He escaped Russia with his family during the Russian revolution. Although my maternal grandfather grew up in a Yiddish-speaking home, he attended a Russian school. After escaping Russia, my mother's family lived first in Vilna, where she was born, then Berlin, and then in Riga, Latvia.

In Riga, my grandfather worked as a salesman and my grandmother Luba, who had studied at a music conservatory in St. Petersburg, worked as a housekeeper. The language spoken in my mother's home was Russian rather than Yiddish, and she attended a German-language high school in which she studied English.

When they met, my parents must have communicated in Russian at first, although my father said that he taught her Yiddish, which became the main language of communication between them.

My father loved my mother unreservedly, but it was clear to me by adolescence that they lived in very different worlds. My mother was much more assimilated into Canadian culture, having friends with whom she communicated and socialized in English.

It was easier for me to connect with my mother as she spoke English fluently. Although she too was preoccupied with her losses, often depressed and frequently distant and unengaged as a mother, I had music in common with her and I admired her outspokenness, her musical talent, and her sense of humor. I was barely an adult when I lost my mother and losing her affected everything going forward. I could not see her clearly. I identified with her and idealized her.

I found the first poem dedicated to my mother very early in my project in the first book I read, *A Zemer fun demer* (A Melody from the Evening), which came out in 1991, twenty-one years after my mother's death. I was surprised to find this poem dedicated to her in this book, because my father had been in a happy and solid third marriage by this time for fifteen years. He refers in this poem to her death "so many years ago," indicating the poem had been written recently.

The poem is entitled "*Lyoln, der muter fun mayne kinder*" (To Lola, the Mother of My Children). The poet speaks of my mother arriving at his bedside at one in the morning, bathed by moonlight at the border between the otherworld and this one. He notes her appeal and charm, which he remembers whenever he closes his eyes, even though it has been so many years since her death. He describes his grief, heavy as a stone, which cannot melt into tears.

After I finished reading all of my father's love poems, it seemed significant that he had written and placed this poem about my mother in the last book he wrote. Seventeen years before, a poem about her ending the book *Shures shire* had a very different tone. It was cold and unforgiving. I thought perhaps that he felt the need to correct his previous last word on their relationship.

That my father grieved after my mother's death was always clear and obvious. But he kept his grief buttoned up, contained within himself and mostly unexpressed outwardly, except for one occasion I still remember vividly.

My mother died suddenly, shortly after a heart attack, when she was fifty years old. In the hospital corridor, when the doctor came out of my mother's room to tell us that she had died, my father sat in dignified silence and simply nodded. A few days later, in the middle of the night, I heard him erupt into out-of-control sobbing. I was shocked because I had never heard my father (or anyone) cry like this before, sobs of unimaginable grief.

None of us living together at the time—I, my brother, and my father (my sister was living in Israel at the time)—referred to this event in the days and years to come. My siblings and I grew up in a family where grief was not openly expressed by our parents. We did not know how to turn toward one another to offer comfort. Our pain about my mother's death was held inside, each of us coping in our own way.

My father's pain was kept in a container locked away from his children. But it was poured, as was everything, into his writing. The section of poems entitled "*Farfrorene trern*" (Frozen Tears), published a few years after my mother's death, was subtitled "*Mayn lyolen*" (To My Lola). Lola was my mother's Russian name, the name by which her closest family and friends knew her. These are the poems he wrote in the years immediately after she died. There are twelve poems, undeniably heartfelt, undeniably beautiful, raw in their expression of love and loss.

Almost every poem made me weep, with vivid visceral depictions of emptiness, grief, loneliness, and the loss of security. I realized, reading through these poems—each one of which I was reading for the first time at the age of seventy-three (all but one of which my father wrote between his ages of sixty-two and sixty-six)—that I was looking for something. I wanted to know specifically what he loved about her.

That my father adored my mother was clear to everyone who knew them well, including their children. In a sense, however, none of these poems is about "her." I didn't read anything about her creativity, her sense of humor, her vanity, her quirkiness, her intelligence, her emotionality. I read that my father missed her physicality—her presence next to him, her arms around his neck—but nothing about her inner qualities, only his. Perhaps his visceral grief for her missing presence overshadowed everything else. Yet I wondered whether my mother felt loved but not known by my father.

In one of these poems, my father's words about allowing his tears to speak consoled me. It seems that when my father's tears did flow, they offered him some relief. I also came to understand how alive everything became for him at night: a potent mixture of his memories, grief, and everything else that inspired his writing.

And then, set in the middle of these poems, I found a mysterious poem that posed a question for the reader. I read it with a mixture of admiration and unease. It is called "*Un vider*" (And Again) and it reads:

And again, a short letter
disturbed the peace in my depths,
and tore me apart—
my wife.

And again, I walk around—a fool—
and feel how pain is devouring me,
and how my body is drying up—
my wife.

> And my intense shame is only for myself,
> that I cannot, I cannot understand you,
> And I walk around blind from suffering—
> my child.

I will never know who sent this note or what was in it. The title—"And Again"—only tells me that this event or one like it had occurred before. I surmised that my father received some information about my mother, and the words that he used about himself in response—"a fool" and "shame"—imply a betrayal, likely an affair.

I had known that my mother had an affair. I was told about it after her death by her closest friend and by my cousins, Peter and Serge, the sons of my mother's brother Grisha. But I had always assumed that my father was ignorant of this fact during his lifetime. My mother had a love affair with a man whom she had known before the war, during her girlhood in Riga. He had been a friend of her older brother Grisha. It seems that the longing for home can be expressed in many different ways.

I was angry on my father's behalf, that the burden of this information added to his suffering. I was angry at the person who sent the information, as I could not imagine any purpose for sending, other than the deliberate desire to cause pain. I had deep compassion for my father's sense of shame at not being able to understand his wife and her actions. I wondered again if his inability to understand her, as he wrote in the poem existed in her as an ongoing frustration and a need.

But at the core, I felt admiration for my father as to where he landed: not in anger, but in pain, confusion and even forgiveness. Over the years, and in his writing, I had seen and read my father expressing plenty of anger, sarcasm and resentment. He did not direct any of this at either the sender or my mother.

"And Again" is the sixth of the twelve poems in this section, placed exactly in the middle and surrounded by pages that express only grief and mourning.

In 1976, six years after my mother's death, my father remarried. His new wife Saba Fried, like him, was a widow, Holocaust survivor and Yiddishist. As my brother Rami said, "She was very good for him." I remember Saba saying on more than one occasion that she had always wanted to marry a poet.

As I approached the last sections of my project, I decided to end on a section of love poetry. I imagined this would be a joyous affirmation, a final chapter in which I could console myself that this is where my father landed. In reality, this was not the last book he wrote, but rather the last one I read. And as I was to discover, the complicated reality of my father's feelings found their way into his love poetry as well. That my father's and Saba's relationship was indeed a joyous affirmation was clear to me but there were bumps along the way, as his poetry describes.

My father and Saba married in 1976. Neither my sister, my brother nor I are very clear on how long Saba and my father knew each another before we were introduced. My brother, who was twenty-one years old and still living at home, told me that one day my father let him know that he had fallen in love. Rami doesn't remember my father ever spending a night away from home, and my father and Saba only lived together after they were married. I recall meeting Saba only a few months before they married.

My father describes his and Saba's courtship with all its infatuation, elation, missteps, doubts and insecurities. I imagined my father reading each of his poems to Saba. He liked to read his poems to others, and it was clearly a way for him to share his feelings.

A frage (A Question) opens this section, dated July 7, 1975. I am unsure why some poems are dated, when the vast majority of them are not. Some may have pointed to an event or time which made an impression and the date may have marked it for the person for whom it was intended.

He opens by asking whether she understands the meaning of the violin melody that is both revealing and asking something, that melody "which weeps in the heart of a poet." He writes that the melody of joy becomes sad because days "fade like tulips" and years lead to the gates, on the other side of which there is no longer any joy. He claims joy is sitting next to her with their hands clasped, yet he carries on his forehead the creases of years which separate them.

He is unsure whether he should dazzle her with everything that is within him, because summer will inevitably be absorbed by the autumn. The violin's melody has passed away in tears, the bow has played him like a cello. Feelings and desires have welled up and stars have been extinguished. Words with which to translate "foggy premonitions" have failed him. He closes with these two lines:

> You sit examining the music
> but have you really understood the violin?

My father is asking Saba whether she understands his fears about their age difference. He feels his happiness and desire, but he has concerns that their age difference will have an impact on their relationship. My father likened himself to a violin, which could play a joyful melody but which trailed off into sadness. There is sadness within him as his years are leading him to the inevitability of death.

I liked that my father thought about Saba and what their life would be like together as he aged. When they were together, neither I nor my siblings knew what the age difference between them was. Saba was fifteen years younger than my father, a bigger difference than we had thought. It appears that this was deeply troubling to him as they began to navigate their relationship.

There are several poems following this first one that express this concern as well as other hesitations and fears. And like my father's other poems, many of his love poems describe both his affirmation and hope, as well as the shadows and fear that forever accompanied him.

In kinozol (In the Movie Theatre) appears to have been written towards the beginning of their relationship. In it, my father describes sitting in a movie theatre with Saba, silent but holding hands. Something had eased between them, he thought. Her fingers were speaking to him in the silence, but he could not yet decipher their meaning just as she didn't hear his speechless emotion. "So let us sit together, thoughtful," he writes. "It's good to sit like this, as a pair." Her expressive fingers smooth out the wrinkles from his forehead and blood. Two striking lines follow: "From love, old hearts become younger, from friendship, bad people become good."

On the movie screen, dreams are extinguished and happiness is mixed with grief and anguish. It is that way between them also, as a new possibility of happiness develops and braids their fingers together. But deep within him a mute sadness arises and he searches her face. He points to their age differences, describing himself as "autumn" and Saba as "summer." He is afraid of disappointment. His half-greyed head and his thoughts set on fire by his ardour are like a red tree in the autumn, alive with colour but signalling the approach of winter.

The poem is full of my father's desire, hopes and fears. It was a time of questioning, in which the nature of their relationship was not quite clear, likely the beginning when they were considering the possibilities of being a romantic couple. He was worried about the age difference between them, about allowing himself to hope and fearing the pain of potential rejection.

A poem entitled *A shotn* (A Shadow) reveals my father's knowledge of his own inner dynamics which he then generalizes to others. He opens the poem by describing a "sickness" that is difficult to heal, a sickness of thought that comes at twilight and creates a story that has little to do with reality. He claims that people carry within themselves specks of dust that have not been swept out and are therefore prepared to believe in the truth of every angry word, unfriendly glance, and kind of foolishness.

He believes that a person can become too comfortable and complacent such that happiness begins to bore him. Therefore, he goes looking for a suspicion which then wells up and eats at him. He tortures himself with these doubts and suspicions and doesn't stop replaying them in his mind.

It is like that inside himself, he confesses at the end of the poem. He spins foolishness. His head speaks sense, his blood sows poison, and he is in the middle. He closes by acknowledging that his life is now too bright, good, and successful, so something gnaws at him and catches a shadow.

I was impressed with my father's self reflection. He understood that he spun a false and negative narrative out of very little information. He was correct in his assumption that we all have sensitivities that remain inside of us, and we can attribute negative motives to others out of these personal vulnerabilities. But I disagreed with his conclusion that it is too much comfort and happiness that creates boredom, leading people to seek drama.

Rather than comfort and complacency, as he conjectured, perhaps a longstanding vulnerability to criticism and rejection (multiplied by the events of his life and his experiences as an immigrant) created the "specks of dust" described in the poem. Additionally, I imagined his father's devout and moralistic nature would have clashed with my father's modern leanings. I imagined that my father never received his father's acknowledgment or recognition for his creative gift.

I've thought about my father's sensitivity to criticism, and his hypersensitivity to an angry look or unkind word. In March 2023, when I travelled to New York to read the letters Chaim Grade had sent him, I also found an unsent letter from my father to Avrom Sutzkever, which described this dynamic perfectly. In this unsent letter, he expressed his offence at Sutzkever's misconstruing a question my father asked about available financial resources for publishing his next book as a direct request for money. [1]

Although my father was sensitive to criticism, a trait that would surely complicate a romantic relationship, he seemed to be more forgiving of empathic failures from women than from men, a dynamic which might have mirrored his relationship with his own mother and father, as described in his poetry and as he recounted personally.

A short and startling poem titled *Reyd* (Talking) reveals a lot about my father's expectations of a romantic partner:

1. For more about Sutzkever, see chapter 8.

Must one explain oneself in words?
That is not good; it is not good.
What speaks is a tear-filled glance.
What speaks are desires
shimmering in the blood.

Words are often lies,
or cover a cryptic message
from hidden melodies
which sparkle
at the bottom of a well.

Don't ask me! I will not speak.
Let us sit quietly . . .
If you can't differentiate
and interpret my silences
how will talking help?

My father speaks of his wish that his deepest and most vulnerable feelings—grief and sexual desire—can be understood without needing to put them into words. Doesn't an ardent glance speak, the poet wonders? Don't tears speak?

His desire for intuitive understanding is probably universal and even necessary to our well-being as young children when we lack the ability to express our needs in words. Yet I found it startling that my father, who revealed his deepest sorrows and most ardent longings through his poetry, would discredit the power of words to clarify meanings and heal misunderstandings in a relationship.

My mother was intuitive and emotional, and in the arena of discerning feelings was probably a good match for my father's needs. But it seems, at least in the beginning of their relationship, that Saba, who was a better match in understanding and supporting my father's life's purpose, found it difficult to read his feelings.

It appears that she wanted him to talk about things he thought she should intuitively understand, and my father was unwilling to expose his vulnerable feelings in conversation. As for words being covers and cryptic messages from unspoken depths, perhaps he did not trust at this point in the relationship that those words in their conversation would be direct and truthful. It seems that my father questioned whether their relationship would be romantic or platonic. He confessed his sexual longing in several poems along with his deep hurt when his hints and physical approaches seemed to be rejected.

In a poem entitled *A shpigele* (A Mirror), my father confesses to Saba that he wasn't honest with her when she called one day to question him about his silence and withdrawal following an outing together. He begins the poem by talking about a mirror in his heart, which has always reflected beauty. This mirror is elevated by a summer's day spent with her, but then the day clouds over. He confesses everything, with perfect honesty, including all the things he couldn't say to her when she asked:

> I was ashamed having grey hair to tell you
> that my heart was forcing a foolish idea.
> So I told you that a sudden pain in my foot
> started to bother me.

> You raised your dark eyebrows
> and asked me, half laughing, coming to your logical conclusion
> —whether you were required to take me in your arms
> and smooth the pain in my foot.

> I didn't answer, but my pierced heart
> shattered into glass splinters.
> The mirror in my heart broke.

He closes by saying:

> It's true that my heart was pierced
> But I have recovered from my vexation.

Admittedly, Saba's teasing rejoinder to my father's claim of a pain in his foot was not the most sensitive response to the vulnerability he was feeling but could not express. People like my father who are afraid to confess vulnerability fear this exact kind of response—being mocked, misunderstood, or denied, rather than embraced and reassured. Saba could not have known what he was feeling and was unwilling to express. He wanted her to intuit it without words.

The poem that closes this section is also the last poem in this book. It is entitled *Kharote* (Regret). This is a difficult poem to write about but omitting it would be a failure to live up to the standard of emotional honesty to which my father aspired.

In this piece, he speaks to someone who could only be my mother. He tells the reader that the light in his torches have burnt out, and all that remains are two tears upon her face and her teary lips, which repeat her last words by the door: "You will understand and you will forgive, when you understand what I'm saying." Two disturbing lines follow:

> I have been faithful for a lifetime
> You—not even one day

He continues:

> How long can one who was made a fool of
> love the one who fooled him?

He returns to the portrait of my mother's face, full of regret, saying:

> Yesterday is already distasteful to you
> but today it is already too late.

He closes the poem by reiterating the first verse. The light in his torches have burnt out and all that remain are two tears upon her eyelashes.

I was troubled by this poem because it didn't jibe with my recollection of what I saw and felt in the days, months, and years after my mother's death. The line about my mother not being faithful to my father even one day is exaggerated and unfair.

There may have been a real conversation between them as this poem implies or it may have been an imaginary one. What I know with certainty is that my father was heartbroken when my mother died and for years afterwards. I believe that my father (as I did) only found out about my mother's affair after she was no longer alive. It's possible that the scenario described in this poem was constructed in my father's imagination after he received and lived with this information for a while. And, perhaps, his new marriage in a loyal and loving union both allowed and required him to say goodbye to one love and to turn wholeheartedly in the direction of another.

Its placement at the end of this book closed a chapter in his life and makes a statement about moving on with a clear conscience. But he corrected this statement about his relationship with my mother in his final book, in the poem *Lyoln, der muter fun mayne kinder* (To Lola, The Mother of my Children), as noted at the beginning of this chapter.

I reserved for myself the privilege of ending this chapter with a poem celebrating the love between my father and Saba and love in general. It is dated October 18th, 1978, inscribed "To Saba" and entitled *Nokh a yor* (Another Year). It acknowledges the anniversary of two years of their married life and reads as follows:

> Two years have already raced away so quickly.
> It seems that we have only just met.
> It seems only yesterday that I was left standing, hypnotized
> by your smile and your charm.
>
> I let my mind wander wonderingly in your gaze
> and saw a brown sun shining there.
>
> Two years have already passed like a myth
> but the sun has not set in your depths,
> it shines golden, beaming—my fortune—
> and it warms my cold winter days.

Every morning, your fingers smooth out my wrinkles.
I become younger, I become big.
I feel your love, I sense your loyalty in my soul
and I hear how my poetry
creates itself in this renewal.

In my sunset days, I thank you silently
with two tears on my eyelashes for this joy
that you carry in your palms for my being—
— two smiling gifts full of light.

Afterword

I often imagine my father as a young man, gazing out his window at night to a clear sky studded with stars, captivated and uplifted by the unfolding of the seasons in the nearby meadows and dancing to the music of the birch tree swaying in his yard. His poetic mind greeted the natural world with awe and wonder.

He found his poetic voice and inspiration in Vilna. I did not know him then, nor did I know him well during his life in Canada. But I know him better now.

I have been immersed in my father's world for more than two years now, and I have been changed by the process. While reading and writing my father's works, his guilt, grief, shame, regret, and joy all resonated within me, but the feeling of aloneness perhaps resonated most. We—my father and I—arrived at this inner aloneness differently, but ultimately it came from the same source: the severance of a people from their home, family, culture, and language.

My guilt and anguish over not knowing my father better while he was alive was very active in me during this time. I fantasized constantly about meeting him on a spiritual plane, during which we could unburden our hearts to one another.

My grief was mostly for him, but also for us, for the conversations that we should have had, for the relationship that was not, for the tragedy of two similar souls missing one other instead of being nourished by the comfort of mutual loss and understanding.

I felt shame and regret for what I didn't see, what I misunderstood, and how I behaved as a result. My father offered me scattered clues about who he was and how he was suffering, but I was too angry about what I didn't receive from him, and too preoccupied with my own pains, to see and take advantage of them.

In 1986, when I was thirty-eight, my father asked me to accompany him to see the documentary *Partisans of Vilna.* This request, like any request he made of me, was unusual and I noted it that way. What I remember most about the documentary were the descriptions of Yiddish cultural life in Vilna, the archival footage of Vilna before the war, and the rubble of destruction afterwards, especially of the Great Synagogue.

Leaving the theater, I noticed that my father looked shaken and pale. He asked me if I had liked the film, and I said yes. I asked him if he had and he too said yes. We walked silently as far as the subway station together and then went our separate ways without further discussion. I have other memories of missed opportunities like this one that I have revisited while reading my father's poems. They sit differently inside me now, with different questions surrounding them.

As much as my father revealed in his poetry and fables and as much as I have learned, I am still left with questions. So many poems for example refer to his "dream," but the dream is never clearly spelled out. At various times, I thought that perhaps the dream was about being published in English, or about the continuity of Yiddish literary culture, or about writing a poem that was finally "fully expressed." It's possible that the dream was all of these things at different times. Whatever his precise dream was, I learned from my father how important it is to have a dream, how a mission, no matter how tragic and impossible, can keep one alive.

There are other things that I learned in reading my father's poetry, noting that this is not an exhaustive list. I learned about the unique artistic and spiritual beauty of Vilna. I learned about my father's literary peers and mentors. I learned about the power of mentorship. I learned about the power of home. I learned about the sustaining power of a righteous cause. I learned the names and personalities of some of my father's relatives. I learned how important a community is to healing. I learned new things about my father, up to and including in the very last poem I read. I learned that my father was trying to communicate with me in his own way.

Most importantly, I learned about my father himself. In baring his soul, he helped to make mine more whole. It seems we need to know where we come from, to which tribe we belong. My father's poetry encouraged me to embrace my first and lost language, Yiddish, and reconnected me to my tribe, the tiny corner of the Jewish community to which I belong, the one that still clings to the language that described and expressed the richness of a thousand years of Jewish life in Eastern Europe.[1]

The poem that started my search, which led me to read his five books of poetry and fables, was not in any of my father's books. The poem was entitled "*Kinder mayne*" (My Children), and it was printed in the *Forverts* newspaper, most likely after my father's last book was published.

To my surprise, this poem was brought to the meeting of a Yiddish conversation group I was attending by Khane Berman, the original seeker of this poem, while I was still reading my father's poetry day by day. I remembered the poem once I saw it. As was typical of my father and of our relationship, he had shown me a copy of it, but we never discussed it together.

The poem asks who will inherit the Yiddish language when he is gone. He remonstrates with himself and wants his children to know that his conscience has tortured him for years for his failure to instill this beautiful language within us. He closes by saying.

> Jews and Yiddish are as bound together
> as an infant at her mother's breast.
> Without one's own language, what also disappears
> is the soul of the Jewish people
> who remembered well and observed
> the origin of a thousand miracles.
> My children, I beg you not to forget
> all the holy things that I am taking with me.

1. Katz, "Yiddish."

The psychoanalyst Michael Eigen is quoted as saying, "The wound that never heals meets the fire that never goes out."[2] There are innumerable wounds that never heal in this world, and many conflagrations that stem from them. Because my father was a poet, his fire burned on the page. It did no damage there, and it did him and others a lot of good. It did me a lot of good.

If I could, I would ask my father's forgiveness for everything I didn't understand, for my blindness and insensitivity. I know if that were possible, he would forgive me and also beg my forgiveness for his lapses and failures. We would embrace one another, and for a time, be at peace.

2. Eigen, *Kabbalah and Psychoanalysis*, vi.

Biographies of Key Figures[1]

E miot, Israel (1909–1978). Born in Poland, published twelve volumes of Yiddish poetry from 1932 to 1969. Fled to the Soviet Union when Germany invaded Poland in 1939. Worked there as a journalist, arrested and convicted of trumped-up crimes, and sentenced to ten years of hard labor in Siberia. Emigrated to the United States in 1958 and lived in Rochester until his death.

Glatshteyn, Yankev/Glatstein, Jacob (1896–1971). Born in Poland, immigrated to New York in 1914. A founding member of the Yiddish modernist group *In zikh* (Introspectivism). Wrote thirteen books of poetry and three novels. Experimented extensively with the Yiddish language, testing its limits. Considered one of the most important Yiddish writers of the twentieth century.

Glik, Hirsh (1922–1944). Born in Vilna. Poet and musician, cofounder of poetry group *Yungvald*, author of the "Partisans' Hymn." Partisan, died in combat against the Nazis.

Gurin, Moshe (1921–1990). Born in Vilna. Poet, cofounder of *Yungvald*. Survived imprisonment in the Vilna ghetto and several concentration camps. Immigrated to Israel in 1947. A member of the writers' group Yung-Yisroel (Young Israel).

Goldkorn, Yitshok (1911–1988). Born in Poland, survived the war by "moving constantly." Poet, essayist, fable writer, and

1. Biographies sourced from yivoencyclopedia.org, except for Hertz Grosbard, which was sourced from grosbardproject.com, and Leivik, H., sourced from encyclopedia.com.

journalist. Lived in Canada from 1951 to 1969, settling in New York until 1977. News editor of *Der Keneder Adler* (The Canadian Eagle, Canada's leading Yiddish newspaper from 1907 to 1977) in Montreal, staff writer at *Forverts* (The Forward) in New York.

Grosbard, Hertz (1892–1994). Actor, performing solo Yiddish "word concerts" to great critical acclaim throughout Europe, the Americas, and Israel. Lifelong promoter of the fables of Eliezer Shteynbarg. Was performing in Buenos Aires in 1939, three weeks before the outbreak of the war. Moved to Canada in 1951 and to Israel in 1971, continuing to perform word concerts until two years before his death at the age of 102.

Grade, Chaim (1910–1982). Born in Vilna. Poet and novelist, acclaimed both for his depictions of Jewish spiritual life and the daily life of ordinary Jews in Vilna. Considered among the most important Yiddish writers of the twentieth century. Survived the war in the Soviet Union, emerging as a defining Yiddish voice in Holocaust literature. Immigrated to the United States in 1948.

Kahan, Shimshon (Syomke) (1905–1941). Born in Vilna. Poet, cofounder of *Yung-Vilne.* Assistant editor and regular contributor to *Vilner tog* (Vilna Day). Murdered in Ponar, 1941.

Kaczerginski, Shmerke (1908–1954). Born in Vilna, poet, musician, and influential cultural activist. A member of *Yung-Vilne.* Imprisoned in the Vilna ghetto, helped to preserve Jewish cultural works as member of the Paper Brigade. Escaped from the Vilna ghetto to fight Nazis as a partisan. Post-war collected and published over 250 Holocaust songs. Moved to Argentina in 1950. Died in a plane crash in 1954.

Korn, Rokhl (1898–1982). Born in east Galicia, Poland, raised on a farming estate. Poet and short story writer, acclaimed for her lyrical style, focus on nature, and characterizations of Jewish and non-Jewish farmers. Survived the war in the Soviet Union. Settled in Montreal in 1949.

Kulback, Moyshe (1896–1937). Born in Smorgon, near Vilna. Poet, novelist, and dramatist. Lived in Minsk and Berlin before returning to Vilna in 1923. Influential and popular figure in Yiddish cultural life, teacher and lecturer. Moved to Soviet Minsk in 1928. Arrested and executed in 1937 in a wave of Stalinist repression.

Leivick, H. (1888–1962). Prominent Yiddish poet and dramatist. Born in Belarus, arrested for distributing revolutionary literature in 1906. Denounced the government at trial, sentenced to forced labor and exile in Siberia. Assisted to escape and reached the United States in 1913. Member of *Di Yunge*, deeply interested in spiritual and messianic themes.

Leyeles, Aaron (1889–1966). Born in Poland, left in 1905, settling in New York in 1909. Poet, educator, journalist, and literary critic. A cofounder of *In zikh* (Introspectivism).

Manger, Itsik (1901–1969). Born in Czernowitz, present-day Ukraine. Poet and playwright, famous for his folk ballads and a new genre, Bible songs. Lived in Warsaw, forced to leave Poland in 1938. Lived in London, New York, settled in Israel, where the Itsik Manger Prize for excellence in Yiddish literature was established in his name in 1988.

Mani Leib (Brahinski) (1883–1953). Born in Russia. Emigrated to the United States, settled in New York in 1906. Poet, a leading member of *Di Yunge* (The Young), the first major literary movement of Yiddish poetry in America, seeking to replace traditional themes and forms of Yiddish poetry with freer artistic expression.

Markish, Peretz (1895–1952). Lived in Kiev, Warsaw, returned to the Soviet Union in 1926. Cofounder of *Literarishe bleter* (Literary Pages) in Warsaw. Broad literary range, lyric and epic poet, novelist, playwright. A founder of expressionist movement in Yiddish poetry. The only Yiddish writer awarded the Order of Lenin. Arrested in 1949, imprisoned, sentenced to death and executed in 1952.

Molodowsky, Kadia (1894–1975). Born in Belarus, prolific and influential poet, essayist, novelist, teacher, and educator. Wrote on political, feminist themes, founded two Yiddish literary journals. Settled in New York in 1935.

Olitski, Leib (1897–1975). Born in Poland, fled Nazi invasion to Russia during World War II, where he spent the war years.

Novelist, fabulist, and poet. Returned to Poland in 1946. During his years in Russia and Communist Poland, he translated Pushkin and Krylov and published ten volumes of prose and poetry. Settled in Israel in 1959.

Peretz, I. L. (1852–1915). Born in Poland. Yiddish and Hebrew poet, writer, dramatist, major figure in Jewish cultural renewal through Yiddish. Encouraged collection of Yiddish folklore and its integration into contemporary art, music, and literature. Worked to raise the status of Yiddish as a Jewish national language.

Sholem Aleichem (1859–1916), pen name of Shalom Rabinovitz. Beloved humorist, impassioned advocate of Yiddish, one of the architects of modern Yiddish literature. *Fiddler on the Roof*, a film that introduced Sholem Aleichem to international audiences, is based on Tevye the Dairyman, a series of monologues written between 1984 and 1914 about Jewish life in a village in imperial Russia.

Singer, I. B. (1904–1991). Born in Poland, emigrated to the United States in 1935. Novelist, short story writer, essayist. Wrote and published first in Yiddish, later translated his own works into English with the help of editors and collaborators, achieved worldwide celebrity. Advocated a return to Jewish folk literature and themes. Awarded Nobel Prize in Literature in 1978.

Shteynbarg, Eliezer (1880–1932). Born in Lipkany, Bessarabia. Master of the fable, fables printed in periodicals popularized in dramatic readings. Original protagonists, often animals, angels, or personified Yiddish letters. Ideas were expressed through Jewish religious culture, laws, rites, and customs.

Mendele Moykher-Sforim (Mendele the Book Peddler), pseudonym of S. Y. Abramovitsch (1835–1917). Born in Belarus, acknowledged widely as founder of modern artistic prose in Hebrew and Yiddish. Prolific writer of novels, short stories, essays, and poetry. Preferred mode was satire. Believed that Jewish religious practice needed to be integrated into the natural world.

Sutzkever, Avrom (1913–2010). Born in Belarus. Considered major Yiddish poet of the twentieth century. Member of *Yung-Vilne*. Participated in the Paper Brigade in the Vilna ghetto, saving documents from Nazi destruction. Partisan. Founder and editor of Yiddish literary journal *Di goldene keyt* (The Golden Chain) in Israel, 1949–1995.

Ravitsh, Melekh, pen name of Zekharye Bergner (1893–1976). Born in Poland. Modernist, expressionist poet. Executive secretary of the Association of Jewish Writers and Journalists in Warsaw (1924–1934). Settled in Montreal in 1940.

Reisen, Avrom (1876–1953). Born in Belarus. Poet, short story writer, known for simple and memorable poems, concise plots. Published literary periodicals. Moved to New York in 1911.

Volf, Leyzer (1910–1943). Born in Vilna. Poet, founding member of *Yung-Vilne*. Known for parodies of European and Yiddish writers, avant-garde artistic performances. Mentored the poetry group *Yungvald* (Young Forest), a group of aspiring teenage poets. Died of starvation near Samarkand in 1943.

Vogler, Elkhonen (1907–1969). Born in Vilna. Poet, leading member of *Yung-Vilne*. Combined folk and modern elements to produce original poetry. Orphaned at a young age. Survived World War II in Soviet Russia. Settled in Paris in 1949.

Appendix: Original Poems in Yiddish

מײַן ליד

כּאָטש ס'איז אָרעם מײַן ליד,
ווי אַ ליכט פֿאַר אַ גראָשן,
שמעלץ איך אָן עס אָן טיש
פֿון מײַן ייִדישן לשון,

ניט פֿאַר יזכּור אַ שעה,
ניט ל'פֿנים אַ קדיש.
נאָר אַנטקעגן אַ ברויט
און פֿריש וואַסער אַ לאַדיש...

1950 מאָנטרעאַל

דרײַ טעג

כ'האָב אויפֿן דנאָ פֿון האַרץ דערטרונקענע דרײַ טעג.
דרײַ רעגנבויגנס אָנגעצונדענע אויף כמאַרעס.
און כ'היט זיי ווי אין וויסטעניש די שפּורן פֿון אַ וועג
וואָס פֿירן ערגעצוווּ, ווּ וווּנדערבאַר איז.

און אַז מײַן לעבן וועט – אין בלויקייט פֿון ים אַ שיף –
פֿון פֿאָרט דײַנעם אַן אָפּגעאַנקערטע פֿאַרזעגלען. –
וועל איך אַ פֿרומער דערוויש אין מײַן אייגן טיף
צו יענע טעג פֿאַרשיפֿטע עולה רגל'ען...

ו, 1933‏ווילנע

האַלבע נאַכט

האַלבע נאַכט.
ס'קאָמט לבֿנה אַ בוים אויפֿן ראָג
מיט אַ זילבערנער קעמל.
ס'שלאָפֿט מיַין באַטקע אין פֿלויט,
ווי אַ פֿלעק אין אַ רעמל.
איך ווייש אויס מיַינע אויגן פֿון דרעמל,
צי אַרויפֿעט דעם טאָג אויף מיַין הויט, –
אַ געלאַטעטע העמד,
און איך לויף אין דער ריי נאָך מיַין ברויט.

ס'לייגט די נאַכט פֿלעקן טינט
אויף אַ זילבערנעם גרונט.
ס'קוקט מיט טויזנטער אויגן דער אויבן.
כ'שטיי אין ריי צוגעפֿרעסט צו אַ וואַנט, –
אַ געשלאָגענער הונט,
און איך שפּיגל מיַין עלנט אין פֿינצטערע שויבן.
ס'טאָגט, עס בלויט.
כ'שפּאַן אַלץ נענטער צום ברויט מיט מיַין צעטל
שטרעק צום פֿעצנטערל אויסעט מיַין האַנט
און איך ווייס ניט צי כ'בעט צי איך בעטל...

כ'גיי צוריק מיט מיַין פֿונט
שוואַרצן ברויט.
ווי אַ ווונד
פֿלאַקערט רויט
דער באַגינען.

כ'שפּאַן ווי שיכּור,
ווי פֿויל.
און די פֿינגער,
ווי גיריקע שפּינען
רײַסן שטיקער
און לייגן אין מויל.

———————

זוימט דער פֿרי ווײַסע וואָלקנס
מיט גאָלדענע שטעך.
בלאָנדער טאָג שפּילט אויף מיר און אַרום מיר.
כ'טראָג מײַן טאָג אויפֿן האַלדז צו מײַן צעך,
ווי מײַן בלעכענעם נומער.
איך בין דאָ דאָ
אויף צוועלף שעה
מיט מײַן פֿײַן
צוגעקלעפּט צו וואַרשטאַטן.
עס צעפֿערטלען די פֿענצטערלעך שײַן
דורך די קראַטן.
עס פֿינטלען די מעסערס, ווי פֿלאַמען
פֿון ליכט אָנגעצונדן אין יאָרצײַט
און ס'זיצן די מענטשן, ווי חרובֿע שטאַמען,
פֿון היימישער ערד אויסגעקאָרטשעט.

כ'זיץ אַליין,
ווי אַ שטיין
אויסגעקערט
פֿון דער ערד,
בײַ אַ פֿינצטערן תהום.
איך בין ווײַט, איך פֿלי ווײַט
צו מײַן ווײַב און מײַן קינד,
צו מײַן שטיבל.
איך צעענעם פֿון מײַן נעכטן דעם קאָם
און צעדריבל
און עס וואַקסט אויף דער וועלט, ווי אַ גיפֿטיקער שוואָם,

מײַן פֿאַראיבל...

שפּאַרט די זון איר פֿאַרבלוטיקטן קאָפּ אױפֿן װאַלד אָן,
ס'ברענט די װײַט.
אינעם הױף אױף אַ דראַנג
מאַכט געװאַלדן
אַ גאַנג
און באַפֿרײַט...

כ'שלעפּ מײַן װאָטעגנעם לעבן אַ הײם
צו אַ באַטקע פֿון לײם.
כ'קום אין שטיבל אַרײַן
זאָג; גוט מאָרגן! מײַן עלנט –
די פֿיר שװאַרצע װענט
ניט ס'באַגעגנט דאָס װײַב
מיטן קינד אױפֿן האַנט.
און כ'פֿאַרװאַרף אױף די ענט
מײַן צעבראָכענעם קאָפּ, װי אַ ציגל.
ס'קלאַפּט די האָפֿענונג אָן אין מײַן שױב,
װי אַ טױב מיט צעבראָכענע פֿליגל.
ס'יאָגט מײַן צװײַפֿל איר אָן,
װי אַ שפּאַרבער זײַן רױב.
עס צעשרײַט זיך מײַן װײַ,
װי אַ פֿינצטערע קראָ
אױף אַ חרובן הױף...

כ'זיץ אַ שעה
און זיץ צװײ,
ביז דער שלאָף עפּעס שװערס און מאַסיװס
טוט אַ װאַלגער מיך אױף דער ראָגאָזשע אַ רו טאָן
און איך בעט בײַ דער נאַכט, װי אַ קינד אַ נאַיװוס,
כאָטש אַ חלום אַ גוטן!...

סאַמאַרקאַנד 2491

איך האָב געוואָלט

איך האָב געוואָלט
אַ שטילן לעבן ווי אַ בן-השמשות, –
אָן גלאַנץ, אָן גאָלד.
נאָר מיינע טעג, ווי פּויערים מיט קאָסעס,
זאָלן פֿון דער אַרבעט גיין מיט לידער.
און איך זאָל זיין – דיין רו
און דו –
מיין סידור...

נאָר ס'האָט דער פֿלאַם פֿון שקיעה
אונדזער היים פֿאַרברענט.
אַן אייזערנער בוראַן
איז איבער אונדזער יונגן לעבן דורכגעגאַנגען.
און אויף אַ בוים,
מיין הויפֿיקן קאַשטאַן, –
האָט מען מיין טרוים
צוזאַם מיט מיין משפחה אויפֿגעהאָנגען...

און מיך, אַ שטויבל, האָט דער ווינט
פֿאַרטראָגן איבער ווייטע ים'ען.
וווּ זאָל איך גיין
אַז ווייטן זיינען בלינד,
אַז וועגן האָבן טויזנט צאַמען!

מען זאָגט; ס'איז אויפֿגעשטאַנען שוין די זון.
די פֿעלדער רײַפֿן שוין מיט נײַע שפֿע,
אַז אָפּגעהאָגלט האָבן האָגלען
פֿון טשוגון.
נאָר פֿון מײַן וואָגלען,
איז מיר צו מײַן לעבן שווער צו טרעפֿן.

ס'האָט וואָס צעשפּאַלטן זיך אויף צוויי אין מיר
און ס'קלעקט מיר קיין מעטאַל ניט צו פֿאַרלייטן...
עס טאָפּטשעט אום אַ קאָנטיקער מײַן וויי אין מיר
און ס'וואָיעט, ווי אַ ווינט מײַן רו
אַן אָפּגעריסענע פֿון קייטן!...

וווילנע 1945

אַ פֿראָסט אַ בייניקער סקעלעט.
נעמט קנאָביק שאַרף דעם וואַלד אַרום;
ס'איז פֿינצטער, אימהדיק און שטום.
עס היגלען זיך אין שניי-פֿאַרשאָט,
די טויטע כוואַליעס שטעכל-דראָט.
עס שמעקן בייזע גראָע הינט,
די נאַכט, די שנייען און דעם ווינט.
עס שטייען זעלנער ווי אַ פֿלויט
און האַלטן אין די הענט דעם טויט.
די גרעניץ צווישן לענדער צוויי.
עס קריכן שאָטנס אויפֿן שניי
אַ לאַנגע ריי און נאָך אַ ריי.
פֿון הינטן מאַניעט זיי אַ שליאַך.
אַ פֿייערל, אַ רויך פֿון דאַך,
אַ בעט אין אַ געהייצטן הויז
און זיי, זיי קריכן אַלץ פֿאָרויס.

אַ ליכטל

אויפֿגעשטאַנען איז אין מיטן נאַכט רב יונה.
אָפּגעגאָסן נעגלוואַסער, אָנגעטריפֿט אַ ליכטעלע אַ קלײנע,
און אַוועקגעזעצט זיך אָפּצוריכטן חצות.
טוט אַ ווינטעלע אַ בלאָז
נעמט דאָס ליכטעלע מיט חלבֿ טראָפֿנס וויינען;

אַ געשטראָפֿט איז זי פֿון גורל איר פ, געשטראָפֿט!
אַלץ געחלומט און געהאָפֿט –
אין אַ פֿרײַטיק אָנצוצינדן זיך אַ שבת-ליכט.
וואָלט אַ מאַמעשי אַ שטילע,
מיט צוויי דורכזיכטיקע הענט פֿאַרדעקנדיק ס'געזיכט,
אָפּגעפֿליסטערט איבער איר אַ תּפֿילה.
וואָלט אַ טאַטע קומענדיק פֿון שול
אויף צוויי חלות בײַ איר שײַן
געזונגען קידוש,
און בײַ איר צופֿוסנס אויפֿן שטול,
וואָלט אַ קינד אַ פֿלאַפֿלערל איר פֿלעמעלע באַחידושט.
וואָלט זיך רויק אויסגעברענט איר לעבן, שיכט נאָך שיכט
און וואָלט אויסגעצאַנקט אַזוי ווי ס'איז באַשערט אַ ליכט,
אויף אַ טישטוך, אין אַ לײַכטער...

אָבער דאָ אין מיטן נאַכט אין פֿײַכטער
בײַ אַ וויינענדיקן איכה-ניגון,
ווו אַ חפֿקרניק, אַ ווינטל, קומט איר פֿלעמל וויגן
און אין דרייען אויסבויגן איר גופֿל, –
דאָס איז צופֿיל!

ליבער,
זאָל אַ שטורעם קומען שוין אויף אַלע שטיבער,
און אַ שלײַדער טאָן דעם טיש דעם קרומען,
די מדינה פֿון איר קראַנקן לעבן.
וואָלט איר פֿלעמל זיך אַ וואָרף געגעבן
אויפֿן ספֿר, אויפֿן דיל און וועַנט
און אין שׂרפֿות זיך צעברענט אין רויטע,
אַש זאָל ווערן פֿון דאָס גאַנצע שטעטל!...

"ששששוטה!
טוט אין ספֿר זיך אַ מיש אַ בלעטל,
ווי אַ צינגל אַ צעפֿענטער;
"בעט ניט אויפֿן שטורעם שוועסטער!
אמת
פֿײַערן צעברענט ער,
אָבער ליכטעלעך פֿאַרלעשט ער...

איך בין געווען

איך בין געווען אַ סאָסנעבוים אין וואַלד פֿון גרינע זינגערס,
אַ סאָסנעבוים, אַ פּעכיקער, פֿון ליכטיקן ניטהי.
צום הימל פֿלעג איך אויסשטרעקן די נאָדלדיקע פֿינגערס
און אָנצינדן אין זריחה זיי אַ יעדן אידערפֿרי.

איך האָב צום הויך געצויגן זיך, צום ווּקס פֿון מײַנע זיידעס, –
די זקנים מיט די זונקעפּ און די שאָטנדיקע בערד;
איך האָב מײַן קרוין מיט זיי צוזאַם צעווייגט אויף הימל-הוידעס
און אָנגעבונדן מײַנע פֿיס אָן פּשוטקייט פֿון ערד.

אַרום געשטאַנען איז אַ וואַלד, וואָס האָט גערוישט מײַן לשון,
און אונטן האָט דער דנאָ געגרינט מיט יונגוואַלד און מיט שטשאַוו.
בײַ נאַכט האָט אויף מײַן שויבער זיך אַ שטערנפֿאָל געלאָשן
און שורות אויפֿן קאָפּ געלאָזט מיט סודותדיקן כּתב.

לבֿנה פֿלעגט מיך זילבערן אין רונעכט ווי אַ לירע,
און אָנשפּאַנען ווי סטרונעס מײַנע צווייגן גרינעם סכך.
ווי פֿייגל פֿלעגן נעסטן אויף מיר ווערטער, און אין שירה
האָב איך צעווייגט מײַן יונגשאַפֿט אין געפֿלאַטער פֿון מײַן שפּראַך.

נאָר ס'האָט אַ האַק, אַ רוצחישע, פֿון שטאַם מיך אָפּגעשניטן,
מײַן קאָרעהויט אַראָפּגעשונדן פֿון מײַן בלײַך געביין,
און מיך געלאָזט אַ נאַקעטן, אין פֿרעמדער וועלט, אין מיטן,
פֿאַרקניפֿלט אין אַ דראָטן-נעץ, בײַם זײַט פֿון לעבן שטיין.

כ'בין איצט אַ טעלעגראַפֿן-סלופ אויף שקיעותדיקע פּליינען...
בײַם זײַט פֿון לעבן שטיי איך, אָן די צוווייגן, אַ בעל-מום.
עס וויגן אין מײַן נעכטן זיך די אָפּגעהאַקטע קרײַנען
און ווייַנען הײַנט פֿון מיר אַרויס צום רויקן אַרום.

אַ משל מיט אַן עכברושל

האָט געוווינט אַן עכברושל אין אַ נאָרע
בײַם מלמד נחום אָרע
וואָכן כמה.
אויפֿגעגעסן דאָרט אַ שטיקל חומש
און אַ פּיצל גמרא,
און אַוועק, אַ סבֿרה,
וווינען צו דעם קרעמער אונגער.
ווער וויל אויסציִען די פֿיס פֿאַר הונגער?

בײַ דעם קרעמער איז אַ שפֿע:
מזון מיטן פֿולן לעפֿל,
מעל און צוקער, קעז און רײַז,
און אַן עולם מײַז
און ראַטן —
קיין בייז אויג זאָל זיי ניט שאַטן!

אַז ס'איז פֿול דער מאָגן ,
ווילט זיך עפּעס נאָך.
נעמט דאָס מײַזל זאָגן
תּורה פֿון איר לאָד:
חומש גאָנצע פּסוקים,
פֿון גמרא, חוקים,
דינים, —
אַלץ בחינם.

און דער עולם מײַז
בײַזן עלטסטן גרײַז
צמאָקען מיט די צינגער,
לעקן אַזש די פֿינגער:
אַזאַ מויז, קיין עין-הרע!
איז עס ניט קיין נס פֿון בורא?
אויפֿגעגעסן בלויז אַ שטיקל חומש,
אַ פיצל גמרא,
און עס זאָגט שוין
סתרי תּורה...

רעקלאַמעס

גרינט אַ קיבוץ לעם כּנרת,
וועלכער שפּיגלט זיך אין זון.
שווימט אַ קאַטשקע אום אין טשערעט,
וואַרעמט זיך אין זאַמד, אַ הון.
און דעם שמועס צווישן ביידן
טראַגט אַ שטילער ווינטל אום...
לאָמיר הערן וואָס זיי ריידן:

רעדט די קאַטשקע: כ'בעט דיך זייער
ליבע הינדל, טו דערקלער!
וואָס די הינערישע אייער
זייַנען אַזוי פּאָפּולער?

יעדע מאַמע טוט זיי קויפֿן
אומעטום, אין יעדעס לאַנד,
פֿרעגלט זיי אויף יעדער אויפֿן,
מייַנע נעמט מען ניט אין האַנט...

כאַטש זיי זייַנען פּונקט ווי דייַנע,
מיט אַ ווייַסל און אַ געלבל,
כאַטש איך לייג זיי אויס, דהיינו,
אויפֿן היי אין זעלבן שטעלבל.

פּונקט װי דײַנע זײַנען מײַנע,
און נאָך גרעסער איז מײַן אײ;
לייג איך אויס פֿאַר דיר מײַן טענה:
פֿאַרװאָס קויפֿט ניט קײנער זײ?

שמייכלט הינדע יענטל
און זי פֿרעגט אַזוי:
װאָס-זשע טוסטו ענטל
אײדער לייגסט דײַן אײ?

װאָס זשע טו איך, כ'זעץ מיך
אויף אַ בינטל הײ,
כ'זעץ מיך און איך קװעטש מיך
ביז איך לייג אַן אײ.

און װאָס טוסטו נאָכדעם
טוט די הון אַ פֿרעג:
כ'שטעל זיך און איך גיי זיך
שטילערהייט אַװעק.

ענטעלע קאַסאָקע
מיטן ברייטן נאָז!
לאָבט די געלע קװאָקע;
שװײַגסט און פֿרעגסט פֿאַרװאָס?

איך אַז כ'דאַרף מיך לייגן
זעץ איך זיך ניט פֿויל,
איך פֿאַרמאַך די אויגן,
עפֿן אויף דאָס מויל:

קאָ קאָ, קאָקאָ, קאָקאָ!
מאַך איך אַ געשרײַ:
איך, די געלע קוואָקע,
לײגן גיי אַן אײַ...

נאָכדעם שוין, אַ מילדע,
אַז איך הויב זיך אויף
מאַך איך אַ געפילדער
אויפֿן גאַנצן הויף.

קאָקאָ, אַלע מאַמעס
הערן מײַן געשרײַ...
אַז איך מאַך רעקלאַמעס
קויפֿן זיי מײַן אײַ!

זון, ים, ווינט

די זון האָט צעקנעפלט איר נאַכטהעמד – אַ כמאַרע –
אַ זילבערנע כמאַרע מיט פורפורנע פונקען,
און האָט איר גינגאָלדענע, שטראַליקע מראה
געגומען אין ימיקער טיפֿעניש טונקען.

דער ים, אויפֿגעברויזט ביז זיין אָפּגרונט דעם שוואַרצן,
האָט בלענדן געגומען מיט אַלערליי פֿאַרבן,
ער טראָגט דאָך דעם אָפּשיין פֿון זון אין זיין האַרצן
אַפֿילו, ווען ס'נעמט אים דער שטורעמווינט קאַרבן.

דער ווינט, זיין לאַנגיאָריקער חבֿר אינטימער,
איז אויכעט פֿאַרליבט אין דער זון, אין בלאָנד-געלער,
פֿאַרניגט ער דעם ים ניט איר בלענדיקן שימער,
ווען ס'באָדט זיך די זון אינעם ימיקן קעלער.

זי נעמט אירע גאָלד-בלאָנדע לאָקן צעלאָזן
ביים ים אויפֿן האַרץ און מיט אים קאָקעטירן...
דער ים נעמט אַזש פֿלאַמען אין פֿרי אינעם ראָזן
מיט גרינע סמאַראַגטן און בלויע סאַפֿירן.

דער ווינט ווערט פֿון קינאה אַ ווילדער געוויטער,
ער וואַרפֿט אויפֿן ים זיך מיט שטורעם און שרעקן,
ער וויל נאָר דער נאַקעטער זון דער צעגליטער,
מיט וואָלקנס מיט גראָע דאָס לייב איר פֿאַרדעקן.

נאָר ס'לאָזט עס דער ים ניט, ער שטעלט זיך אַנטקעגן,
אַפֿילו אַ חבֿר, נאָר ליבשאַפֿט איז מערער,
ער וואַרפֿט זײַנע כוואַליעס מיט כעס אין געשלעגן
און וואַליעט און כמאַליעט דעם ווינט – דעם צעשטערער.

נאָר ס'פֿליט אום דער ווינט אויף צעוויכערטע פֿליגלען,
ער רײַסט פֿון ים שטיקער, די זון זאָל זײַן גנאי זען.
ער האָט שוין צעבראָכן אין ים אַלע שפּיגלען,
די זון זאָל ניט קאָנען איר פּנים דאָרט ווײַזן.

די זון קוקט באַהאַלטן אַרויס דורך אַ שפּאַרע
און שמייכלט צו זיך אויפֿן אויבערשטן גאָרן,
עס שלאָגן זיך אונטן צוויי זכרים וואָלגאַרע,
וואָס מיינען, זיי זײַנען דער זונס "אוכאַזשאָרן".

אויף מאָרגן פֿאַרלאָזן וועט זיי דער ירגזון,
דער ים מיטן ווינט וועלן אויפֿהערן רעשן,
און ווידער וועט זי אין פֿרימאָרגן דעם ראָזן
די גאָלדענע האָר אינעם ים קומען וואַשן.

אַ שטורעם

דער ווינט געקומען, אַן אין'כּעס'ער,
איז אויף דער בליִענדיקער ערד.
ער האָט צעמאָלט אויף שוים דעם וואַסער,
פֿון ביינער אויסגעריסן בערד.

די שטיבער האָט ער אויסגעבויגן
און זיי געלאָזן שטיין פֿאַרקערט.
ער איז פֿאַרנאַכט אַװעקגעפֿלויגן,
אַ שטעטעלע האָט ער צעשטערט.

ביינאַכט געפֿינקלט האָבן שטערן,
אַ בשׂורה האָבן זיי געבראַכט:
אַז דאָס וואָס ס'טוט אַ ווינט צעשטערן
וועט ווידער אויפֿשפּראָצן אין פּראַכט.

ווייַל אינעם מענטשן און אין ביימער
און אַלץ וואָס וואַקסט פֿון דר'ערד און גרינט,
ליגט אַזאַ כּוח, אַ געהיימער,
וואָס איז נאָך שטאַרקער פֿונעם ווינט.

די זון אין פֿרי האָט אויסגעוואַשן
די אויגן גאָלדענע מיט טוי.
און האָט גענומען איבעררראַשן
דעם בראָך פֿון שטורעם, ימח שמו!

די גראָזן האָט זי אויפֿגעהויבן
דעם מענטש געוואַרעמט און געטרייסט.
און ווידער אָנגעהויבן גלויבן
האָט אַלץ אַרום פֿון ווינט דערלייזט.

ווייל מיט חלומות און בטחון,
איז אין זיין תּוך דער מענטש געבענטשט,
אַז אַלץ וואָס וועט פֿון ווינט צעבראָכן,
זאָל ווידער אויפֿבויען דער מענטש.

רעגן-בויגנס

די זון זעגט מיט גאָלדענע זעגן
די קעפּ פֿון די כמאַרעס אַראָפּ.
עס שימערט אַ גאָלדענער רעגן,
וואָס טוט מײַנע ווערטער אָן טראָפּ.

אַ ניגון, אַ זעלטענער ניגון,
צעזינגט זיך אין מיר ווי אַ פֿלייט,
און ס'הייבט אָן דאָס האַרץ מײַנס זיך וויגן
אויף ליכטיקע סטרונעס פֿון פֿרייד.

איך גיי אַ פֿאַרקלערטער, פֿאַרהערטער,
און ס'קלינגען בײַ מיר אין געמיט
צעגלימערטע ייִדישע ווערטער
און שטעלן זיך אויס אין אַ ליד.

נאָר קלענער ווער איך אין אַליינקייט,
עס צאַנקט ווי אַ ליכטל מײַן פֿרייד.
אַזאַ, אַזאַ פּשוטע שיינקייט –
און שווער צו פֿאַרטײַטשן מיט רייד.

איך גיי אַ פֿאַרטערערטער, פֿאַרהערטער
אין גאָלדיק צערעגנטן שפּריי;
איך זוך פֿאַר די טראָפֿנדלעך ווערטער,
און ס'פֿעלן מיר ווערטער פֿאַר זיי.

ס׳טרעפֿט

און ס'טרעפֿט איין וואָרט טוט בלויז אַ העל:
עס וועקן אויף זיך שעהען בלויסטע,
עס ווערט דער גוף אַ וויאָלאָנטשעל
מיט סטרונעס ציטערדיק צעברויזטע.
און עמעץ נעמט מיך אָן ביים האַלדז,
און הוידעט איין מיך אין אַזאַ וויג,
אַז טראָפֿנס בלוט און טרערן זאַלץ
זיך זײַנען אויף מײַן דנאָ מזוווג.
און אַלץ ווערט, ווי דער זאַפֿט פֿון מאָן
וואָלט אײַנגעשיכּורט מײַנע חושים –

און ס'ווערט מײַן רעיון אָנגעטאָן
אין ליד און וואָרט ווי אין מלבושים.

מײַן שׂטן

כ'קריג זיך תּמיד אַרום מיט מײַן שׂטן,
כאָטש איך קאָן ניט זײַן פּנים זען קלאָר, –
כאָטש זײַן וועג איז אין מיר אויסגעטראָטן
און ער עלטערט זיך מיט מײַנע יאָר.

יעדע נאַכט וואַקט מיך אויף זײַן געפֿליסטער,
יעדן טאָג גייט ער נאָך מײַנע טריט, –
כ'האָב אים פֿײַנט, דעם פֿאַרהוילענעם נסתּר,
און איך טראָג אים אַרום אין געמיט.

ס'לאַכט מיך אויס זײַן פֿיליסטערשער שמייכל, –
מיך, מײַן נאַרישע האַרץ און מײַן פֿליד...
כ'וועאר מיך אָפ פֿון זײַן סם מיט מײַן שׂכל,
כאָטש איך וווייס, אַז מײַן שׂטן בין איך.

לערן מיך

לערן מיך געדענקען, ניט פֿאַרגעסן
אַלע מײַנע נעכטיקע מעת-לעתן,

אַלע מײַנע אומװעגן אין גיין.

לערן מיך אין װײַטערגאַנג געדענקען
אַלע װילדע שטעגן פֿון מײַן בענקען,
כ'זאָל אין גאַנג דערגיין צו זיך אַליין.

כ'בין געגאַנגען זוכן זון און טרוימען
אין די טיפֿע תּהומען, אין די הױכע רױמען,
אומעטום האָב איך געשיקט מײַן טראָט,

ביז כ'האָב אױף דער עלטער אױסגעפֿונען,
אַז ניט אין דעם אױסגעשטראַל פֿון זונען,
נאָר אין האַרץ פֿון מענטש אַליין װינט גאָט.

בעט איך גאָט צו פֿאָרעמען מײַן לעבן,
כ'זאָל זיך קאָנען ביזן טױט צעגעבן,
אױך מײַן פֿלײש זאָל מיר ניט זײַן קיין שאָד.

לערן מיך, אַז געבן זאָל מײַן פֿרײד זײַן
און אַז געבן זאָל איך תּמיד גרײט זײַן,
איך זאָל װערט זײַן דו זאָלסט װױנען אין מיר, גאָט.

...איך וויל ניט זײַן

אָ, גאָט, איך וויל ניט זײַן קיין פּאָפּוגײַ
און נאָכזאָגן דעם חכמס פּלאַפּערײַ,
כ'וויל שרײַען ווי אַ וואָלף בײַ נאַכט אין שניי
און אויפֿוועקן דעם וואַלד מיט מײַן געשרײַ.

דער וואַלד איז פֿול מיט שוויַיגן און מיט שרעק,
דער ווינטער האָט זײַן העל-גרין לײַב פֿאַרדעקט,
און אין די שאָטנס זײַנע לוֹיערט בלוטיק-רויט,
דער הונגער און די מורא פֿאַרן טויט.

איך וויל ניט זײַן דער יעגער, ניט די ביקס,
אויך ניט דער הירש. כ'וויל זײַן אַ שטיל געוויקס,
וואָס חלומט אין דעם זילבערדיקן פֿליִען
פֿון פֿרילינג, וואָס וועט קומען ווען צוגיִען.

צו רחל קאָרן

פֿאַר איר בוך
"די גענאָד פֿון וואָרט"

אַ מאָל דערהאָרכט מען זיך אין יענעמס ווערטער
און יענעמס ווידוי ווערט אַן אייגן סוד.
איך האָב אין אײַער בלעטערפֿאַל דערהערט זיך,
אַ דאַנק אײַך פֿאַרן זינגוואָרט פֿון גענאָד.

אין שעהען ווען די רגעס ווערן גרויער
און שויבן זײַנען בעלמעדיק און בלינד,
איז קלוג אַזוי צו טרינקען אײַער טרויער
און גליִען ווי אַ האַרבסטבוים אינעם ווינט.

איך גלי מיט אײַער פֿליסטערוואָרט אין אויער,
מיט אײַער טרער, וואָס ברענט און היילט ווי יאָד.
אַ דאַנק פֿאַר אײַער "חשוונדיקן טרויער",
אַ דאַנק פֿאַר אַלע ווערטער פֿון גענאָד.

שטילער

שטילער
טרילער
סאָלאָווייי!
אַלע וועלטן שלאָפֿן.
בלויז אַ דימענטענער שפּריי
שטערנט אין אָנ'סופֿן,

בלויז אַ וואַכער
לאַכער-קוואַל
מורמלט וואָס דעם געגנט.
און אַ גרינער שטערנפֿאַל
רעגנט,
רעגנט,
רעגנט...

1938 ווילנע

דער פֿרילינג - דער מאָלער

דער פֿרילינג, דער מאָלער געהיימער,
אין זוניקן קאַפֿטן,
מאָלט אויסעט אויף זאַמדן און ליימען
די שענסטע לאַנדשאַפֿטן.

ער נעמט זײַן פּאַליטרע – דעם הימל –
אין בלויע פֿאַרטאָגן
און מאָלט אויס אַ בלימל
נאָך שענער פֿון ווינצענט וואַן גאָגן.

ער קוועטשט אין זײַן טובע, –
און ס'הענגט רעגנבויגיק אַ ווונדער.
זײַן פֿענדזל – דעם נעפּל –
ער פֿירט אויף דער לאָנקע דער רונדער.

ער שמירט אָפּ די בערגלעך און טאָלן,
באַשפּרענקלט די טאַנען.
און ס'וואַקסן אויס לײַוונטן
הערלעבע ווי בײַ סעזאַנען.

אַ מאָל, גאָר אַ מאָל, אין אַ שקיעה
באַוווּנדערט דעם מאָלער
איך האָב בײַ דער גרינער ווילִיע,
אויף בערג אַנטאָקאָלער.

הײַנט האָב איך אים ווידער באַגעגנט
אין זונטאָג אין קלאָרן
בײַ זײַנעם אַ בילד, אין אַ געגנט,
לעם גרויסן סענט-לאָרען.

און ווידער

און ווידער האָט אַ קלײנער בריוו
מײַן רו צעװירבלט אין מײַן טיף,
און מיך צעװײַקט רױט און רױ –
מײַן פֿרױ.

און ווידער גײ איך אום – אַ נאַר –
און פֿיל, װי ס'עסט מיך אױף אַ צער,
װי ס'טרינקט אױס אין מיר דאָס לײַב –
מײַן װײַב.

און כ'שעם זיך שטאַרק פֿאַר זיך אַלײן,
װאָס כ'קאָן ניט זיך, ניט דיך פֿאַרשטײן,
און כ'גײ אַרום פֿון װײטיק בלינד –
מײַן קינד.

רייד

דאַרף מען זיך מיט רייד דערקלערן
איז ניט גוט, איז ניט גוט.
זאָגן דאַרף דער בליק אין טרערן,
ריידן דאַרפֿן די באַגערן,
וועלכע שימערן אין בלוט.

ווערטער זײַנען אָפֿט ליגונים,
אַ פֿאַרדעק, אַ פֿאַרדעק
פֿאַר באַהאַלטענע ניגונים,
וועלכע גלימערן אין ברונעם
אויפֿן דעק, אויפֿן דעק.

פֿרעג מיך ניט! איך וועל ניט ריידן,
לאָמיר זיצן שטילערהייט...
אויב דו קאָנסט ניט אונטערשיידן
און מײַן שווײַגן ניט באַשיידן,
וואָס זשע וועלן העלפֿן רייד?

נאָך אַ יאָר

שוין צוויי יאָר אַוועקגעלאָפֿן
אַזוי גיך,
דאַכט זיך, אָקאָרשט אָנגעטראָפֿן
האָט מען זיך.
דאַכט זיך, נעכטן כ'בין געבליבן
פֿאַר דיר שטיין,
פֿאַר דיַין שמייכל פֿאַר דיַין ליבן,
פֿאַר דיַין חן.
כ'האָב פֿאַרקוקט זיך ווי פֿאַרוווּנדערט
אין דיַין בליק
און דערזען, אַ ברוינע זון דאָרט,
שיַינענדיק.
שוין צוויי יאָר אַוועקגעגאַנגען,
ווי אַ מיף,
נאָר די זון איז ניט פֿאַרגאַנגען
אין דיַין טיף,
גאָלדיק שיַינט זי, אַ צעשטראַלטע,
מיַין פֿאַרמעג,
און זי וואַרעמט מיַינע קאַלטע
ווינטערטעג.
יעדן פֿרי, ווען דיַינע פֿינגער
גלעטן אויס
מיַינע קנייטשן, ווער איך יינגער,
ווער איך גרויס.
כ'שפֿיר דיַין ליבשאַפֿט, כ'פֿיל דיַין טרייַשאַפֿט
אין געמיט

און איך הער ווי אויף דאָס נײַ שאַפֿט
זיך מײַן ליד.
דאַנק איך דיר אין מײַנע שקיעות,
שטילערהייט,
מיט צוויי טרערן אויף די וויִעס,
פֿאַר דער פֿרייד
וואָס דו טראָגסט אין דײַנע דלאָניעס
פֿאַר מײַן זײַן –
צוויי צעשמייכלטע מתּנות,
פֿול מיט שײַן.

טאָראָנטע, אָקטאָבער 18, 1978

Bibliography

Blatman, Daniel. "Bund." In *YIVO Encyclopedia of Jews in Eastern Europe*. 2010. https://yivoencyclopedia.org/article.aspx/Bund.

Cammy, Justin Daniel. "Volf, Leyzer." In *YIVO Encyclopedia of Jews in Eastern Europe*. 2010. https://yivoencyclopedia.org/article.aspx/Volf_Leyzer.

———. "Yung-Vilne." In *YIVO Encyclopedia of Jews in Eastern Europe*. 2010. https://yivoencyclopedia.org/article.aspx/Yung-vilne.

Eigen, Michael. *Kabbalah and Psychoanalysis*. London: Karnac, 2012.

Frank, Esther. "Korn, Rokhl." In *YIVO Encyclopedia of Jews in Eastern Europe*. 2010. https://yivoencyclopedia.org/article.aspx/Korn_Rokhl.

Denman, H. "Leyvik, H." In *Encyclopaedia Judaica*. https://www.encyclopedia.com/religion/encyclopedias-almanacs-transcripts-and-maps/leivik-h.

Grade, Chaim. *My Mother's Sabbath Days*. New York: Rowman & Littlefield, 2004.

Katz, Dovid. "Language: Yiddish." In *YIVO Encyclopedia of Jews in Eastern Europe*. 2011. https://yivoencyclopedia.org/article.aspx/Language/Yiddish.

Kuznitz, Cecile Esther. "YIVO." In *YIVO Encyclopedia of Jews in Eastern Europe*. 2010. https://yivoencyclopedia.org/article.aspx/YIVO.

Niborski, Yitskhok. "Shteynbarg, Eliezer." In *YIVO Encyclopedia of Jews in Eastern Europe*. 2010. https://yivoencyclopedia.org/article.aspx/Shteynbarg_Eliezer.

Roskies, D. "Manger." In *A Bridge of Longing: The Lost Art of Yiddish Storytelling*. Cambridge, MA: Harvard University Press, 1995.

Singer, I. B. "Immigration." *Pakntreger*, spring 2020. https://www.yiddishbookcenter.org/language-literature-culture/pakn-treger/2020-pakn-treger-digital-translation-issue/immigration.

Zalkin, Mordechai. "Strashun, Shemu'el and Matityahu." In *YIVO Encyclopedia of Jews in Eastern Europe*. 2010. https://yivoencyclopedia.org/article.aspx/Strashun_Shemuel_and_Matityahu.

———. "Vilnius." In *YIVO Encyclopedia of Jews in Eastern Europe*. 2010. https://yivoencyclopedia.org/article.aspx/Vilnius.